Play the STUDY GAME for Better Grades

Laia Hanau

Fifth Edition

Formerly *The Study Game: How to Play and Win*

BARNES & NOBLE BOOKS
A DIVISION OF HARPER & ROW, PUBLISHERS
New York, Cambridge, Philadelphia, San Francisco
London, Mexico City, São Paulo, Singapore, Sydney

CONTENTS

This is a revised edition of *The Study Game: How to Play and Win*, Fourth Edition.

Library of Congress Cataloging in Publication Data

Hanau, Laia.
    Play the study game for better grades.

    Rev. ed. of: Study game. 3rd ed. 1974.
    Includes index.
    1. Study, Method of. I. Hanau, Laia, Study game.
II. Title.
LB1049.H28   1985   371.3′028′12   84-48845
ISBN 0-06-463715-8 (pbk.)

85 86 87 88 89 10 9 8 7 6 5 4 3 2 1

1

STUDY PROBLEMS

Hello.

I'm the Author.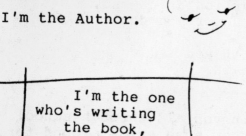

> I'm the one
> who's writing
> the book,

and this is one of my friends

 a student
who wants to
get better
grades in school

> without doing
> a lot of work.

And this

 Hi!

is a Study Problem.
Study Problems are very friendly,
and very clingy,

but that is no reason
to like them.

They keep you from getting
better grades; they make
studying harder for you; and they
cause all kinds of other troubles

 Don't blame me for everything.

✓ miseries
✓ depressions
✓ parent problems
✓ teacher problems
✓ inferiority feelings
✓ future job worries

Just about everybody has them,
of course, except the students who
get good grades easily.

And most of the students who
don't have them in high school
get them in college.

Some Study Problems only stay around
for a few months during a particular course,
or while you've got an Instructor you don't like.

Others just move in on you
as a permanent, live-in
attachment.

They stay with you all through school.
And some of them even stick around for
the rest of your life, making things
hard for you (especially in your jobs).

But all of them, temporary residents
or forever friends,

live together with your grades,
in a sort of permanent see-saw system...

When they go down, your grades go up.

When they go up, your grades go down.

So if you're shopping around
for better grades,

or the same grades with less work,
you have to get rid of at least some of them.

The trouble with Study Problems is that
most people don't recognize one
when they meet one.

You called?

No, I did not.
Go away.

Most people, like
your parents, or teachers, or even
your friends

if they think you've got a Study Problem,

2

they all give you this
kind of advice ⟶

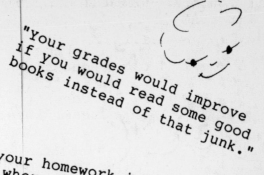

"You'd get better grades
if you didn't watch
so much TV."

"Your grades would improve
if you would read some good
books instead of that junk."

"If you did your homework in
another room where it's quiet,
you'd get better grades in school."

But noise, TV and the books you read
are not Study Problems.

        They are only excuses for not studying.

So, even if you lock yourself in a sound-proof room,
pull the plug on the TV, and make yourself read the
encyclopedia,

        you will have suffered for nothing.
        Your grades won't get any better.

You have to look elsewhere for Study Problems.
You can tell if you've got one
if you hear yourself muttering that

THE INSTRUCTOR

is disorganized.

doesn't explain anything.

throws in unimportant junk.

expects us to memorize useless details.

is a louse.

goes too fast.

gives us too much work.

Or, if you hear yourself complaining
that THE EXAM

. is too long
. questions are ambiguous
. isn't fair
. doesn't let me show what I know
. asks questions on insignificant details.

Exams are unfair to students.

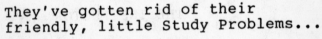

No they're not. Go away.

Or, if you have a vague, miserable feeling
that there ought to be an easier way to
get through school...

.. because you're spending too much time
on studying & still not getting
good-enough grades ??

.. because your grades are okay, but
how-come other people get good grades
and still have time for fun & hanging out ??

"How come" is because those students have figured
out the study game and how to play it.

They've gotten rid of their
friendly, little Study Problems...

and you can, too.

There are two basic types
of Study Problems

| The Sunburn |
| & |
| The Spotty One |

4

The Sunburn is
the all-over type.

.. This is where school work is a
general muddle and mess, and a
lot of work and aggravation, and
a nuisance or an irritation.

People who have this type suffer a lot.

They suffer from misery in school
or they suffer from trying to think up
ways to get out of school work.

But they suffer the most
from what other people say.

People are always telling them (or telling you)
things like,

"Now, Jebelworth, you know if you applied
yourself, you could get good grades!"

Honestly!

If you knew how to do it,
NATURALLY you'd be doing it. Do they think
you're getting rotten grades on purpose??!!

Applying yourself is a very good thing.
I'm all in favor of applying yourself and being motivated.

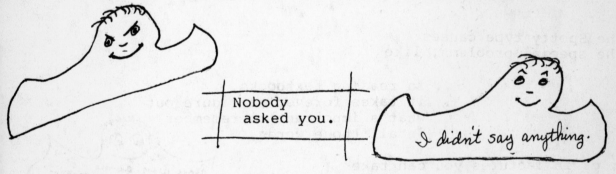

Nobody
asked you.

I didn't say anything.

But if you want the truth of the matter...

there's absolutely no point in gearing
yourself up to being "motivated"

if you don't know
how to go about studying
after you're motivated.

Is there?

5

The other type of Study Problem
is The Spotty One.

.. This is where you can do one kind
kind of school-stuff, but not
another...

. maybe you can do English,
but not Chemistry

. or you can do Science, but
your grades are rotten
in History.

This is the kind that most teachers have.

Oh, yes, teachers have Study Problems.

. Some of them can do English,
but not Math,

so they teach English.

. Some of them can do Science,
but not History,

so they teach Science.

You just don't know about it because you never
saw them as students. In college, their Instructors
knew about it, though. And so did they.

The Spotty type causes
the special problems, like

.. in reading textbooks,
it takes forever to figure out
what's important to remember
in all those words,

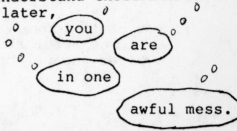

you win some -
you lose some -

.. or in lectures you can take
lots of notes but three weeks
later they don't make any sense,

and if you're like some students
who can't understand their own notes
three DAYS later,

you

are

in one

awful mess.

The worst thing about this Spotty type
is that you're going along feeling you've
got the whole thing licked,

　　　and whammo!

　　　　　　　　　You're smacked with a low grade
　　　　　　　　　in some required course.

　　　　　　　　　　　It's very discouraging,
　　　　　　　　　because
　　　　　　　　　　　you never know why it happens.

Win some, lose some.

The reason for both types
of Study Problems

　　　is that you really don't have an easy,

　　　　efficient, problem-eliminating,
　　　　　　　　　am I both?

　　　　　　grade-getting study system.

You probably go over your textbooks and your notes,
and discuss the stuff with friends, then
read it again...and stare out of windows,

　　　　and hope that somehow everything will
　　　　sort itself out in your head
　　　　at exam time...

　　　　　　　　...which takes
　　　　　　　　　　the whole business
　　　　　　　　　　　of getting grades

　　　　　　　　　　and turns it over
　　　　　　　　　　　　to an inefficient,

　　　　　　　　　　　　patchwork system.

Patchwork study systems...develop...in students' heads...
from one uptight exam...to another....This is...no way...
to run...your life....

　　　　　　　　　⤷ Examples of patchwork systems ⤳

7

There is one that comes from never really knowing where you are in a course, or when you are through studying something.

This one is called the

"What's It All About, Anyway?" system.

This is
a thing
that has
to be
studied.

There is a ⤳ "Check & Re-check" system

where you keep going over and
over the same material.

The idea is that if you understand every piece,
something inside will take over and you will

understand the Whole Thing in the exam.

Very time-consuming. And it never
does fit together into a whole
picture in the exam, or any other time.

In this system

                      □ you read   the paragraph.
          Then you say what   the paragragh   said.
          Then you re-read   the paragraph
       to see if what you said about   the paragraph   was right.
    Then you make up some questions on   the paragraph.
    Then you see if you can answer the
          questions you made up on what
                      you thought   the paragraph   said.
    Then, if you're really doing it
          properly...you will re-read   the paragraph   to see if
          your answers are correct.

          Then I go nuts.

          Because I can't stand repetition.

                Paragraphs, or sections, or chapters...
                I can't stand going over the same thing
                five hundred thousand times!

Don't exaggerate.
Some people like to study that way.

yick!

9

There is the

"Mess Yourself Up" system

that a lot of
students get taught in school.

 It's an inefficient system, but
they get taught it anyway.

First,
you open your book and
Skim the material.

Then you Make Up Questions on the material
you haven't read.

Mess-up number 1.

Then you Read
the material.

You are now reading to answer the
questions you made up,

which closes your mind to what the material
is saying apart from the questions.

Mess-up number 2.

Then you
Re-phrase the
material...

...and how can you possibly know
whether what you say the book is saying

is what the book is saying ???

, Mess-up number 3.

It doesn't
give them A's or B's.

For your exam
you Review it all, and memorize what you can.

The problem is...you can memorize forever,
but who knows whether what
you're memorizing is correct??

10

There is a system that comes from going over & over notes;
underlining lines & lines in textbooks,

    then reading and re-reading the underlines;

        and in between talking & talking bits and
        pieces over and over with friends.

It is called the

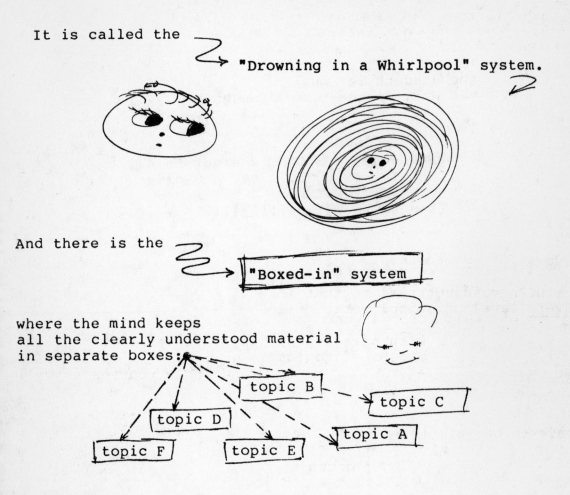

        "Drowning in a Whirlpool" system.

And there is the

"Boxed-in" system

where the mind keeps
all the clearly understood material
in separate boxes:

topic B

topic C

topic D

topic A

topic F

topic E

It can send a student into
a screeching frustration at
exam time.

        He did his homework every day,
            and he really does understand every topic.

But his study system
doesn't know how to organize
the topics and fit them together

      so that he can find the Big Picture
        the exam questions are asking for....

His friends came to him before the exam,
and he sat on the floor with them

>   and answered all their questions. He
>   cleared up all the fuzz-areas in the
>   topics they brought up.

Then they all took the exam
together. When they got their
papers back,

>   the student let out
>   the Wail-of-the-Miserable-Ones,

>   "How come, HOW COME she got an A
>   and I, HOW COME, I get a C-plus
>   when I TAUGHT her
>   the WHOLE THING??!!*%#?!??"

"How come..." is because

the student did not realize that
at <u>every</u> level of school work,

>   with paragraphs, single topics,
>   groups of topics,
>   and whole courses as well,

you have to be able to

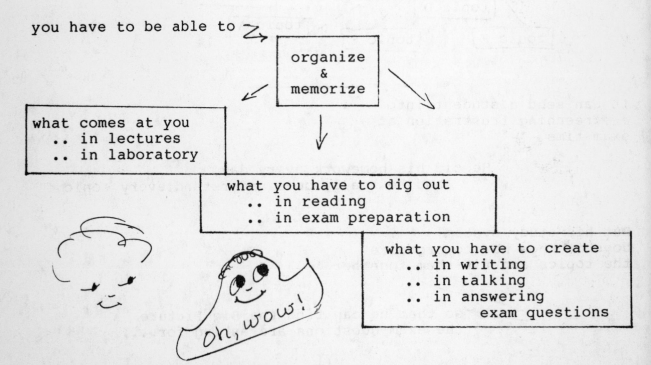

organize
&
memorize

what comes at you
.. in lectures
.. in laboratory

what you have to dig out
.. in reading
.. in exam preparation

what you have to create
.. in writing
.. in talking
.. in answering
            exam questions

oh, wow!

That's what school work is.

After you follow the basic rules for getting good grades,

...go to class, turn in homework, take
the exams, & be polite to teachers,

you have to know how to organize and memorize what comes
at you, what you have to dig out on your own, & what you
have to create out of your head. These are the school jobs
that everyone has to deal with.

And inefficient study systems will splither
into mush-puddles as you proceed through
the school system

→ grade school
↓ high school
↓ college
↓ professional school

because

. the amount of stuff you have to learn gets greater,
. the chance to review topics in class drops to zero,
. the competition gets tougher
  and
. the grading gets harder.

The result is you have
less & less time to get the work done

and come up with
the grades you want.

You don't need to get A's in school
to succeed in life, you know.

If you want A's, that's fine. If you want B's,
that's fine. If you want C's, that's also fine.
(D's, E's or F's are not fine.)

All you need is to know
how to study,
and how much to study,

to get the grades you want.

And that is easy to learn.

Wanna
watch MTV?

Studying isn't hard.
It isn't a mystery, and it isn't magic.

It's just a thing to learn how to do,
like swimming, or playing the piano.

It's a game you play
in school.

Easy to learn and easy to win.

The students who get good grades easily,

the ones without Study Problems...
the ones who know how to play the study game...

just happened to stumble onto
these techniques for studying,
somewhere along the school line,

just as you stumbled upon this book,

because

what this book is going to do is

show you how to do it, too.

(Why should <u>they</u> know how to do it, and you not?)

2

The first technique you need
shows you how to take great notes.

Did anyone ever tell you
that for school work,

knowing how to take great notes
that you can understand 3 months
(or even 3 years) later

is more important than
reading well?

It happens that way because
taking great, first-class notes

(first-class notes -- not the
outlining and keyword stuff)

keeps training your mind to read faster & better.

But reading faster & better doesn't train
you to take first-class notes, does it?

This first-class note-taking
is like a nice, luxurious
Cadillac...rolling you smooth as silk,
right along into better grades.

With this technique you can organize anything
and everything, from paragraphs to whole
courses, in all kinds of subjects, and for
all kinds of Instructors.

Nice, huh?

So, let's begin with

what every good student knows

To take notes you have to know this:

EVERYING

written
or
spoken

IS MADE UP OF ONLY TWO ELEMENTS.

When anyone writes or
speaks that person has
to use one or the other
or both. Mostly both.

I call these elements

Statement

and

Pie

and the letters of P I E  stand for the words

P ... Proof
I ... Information
E ... Example

But, now that you know where the letters in PIE
come from,

don't waste time figuring out whether
some item is a "proof", or a piece of
"information", or an "example"

because minds are different; and
some item that you (or your
Instructor) decide to call
PROOF, another Instructor will
decide to call EXAMPLE.

...And I'm the type who would
probably call it INFORMATION.

So it is easier to just call
any item ———> Pie.

You see, it really doesn't make any
difference what a person thinks about
any item.

Your mind can call
any item anything
it wishes:

example, proof
or information...

these are only
different words
for an item.

17

At this point you don't believe the stuff about
Statement-Pie (St-Pie)....

Anyway,
I <u>hope</u> you don't believe me,

since that will prove

you have a mind
not a sponge
in your head.

The reason for not believing it
is that you have not been given
any proof (P)

that it is correct,

nor enough information (i) about it for you to
decide whether it is true or not . . .

. . . nor enough examples (e) for you
to decide anything about anything.

So you don't accept my Statement:

"Everything, written or spoken, can be
broken into two elements: Statement & Pie"

because

you have

not been

given any

Pie for

it

which, of course, just
proves how IMPORTANT
the Pie is.

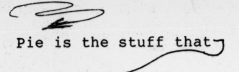

Pie is the stuff that

    makes someone believe what you said.

    It makes your reader or listener believe your Statement.

We are not discussing
whether your Statement
is true or not. Let us
deal with first things first.

For instance:

    You say to your parents: "All the kids are going
hang-gliding this weekend."

                    That is your   STATEMENT

To get your parents to believe it -- so you can go
hang-gliding, too -- you name Johnny, Joe, Josephine, Jim
and Icarus who are going hang-gliding.

So

        - Johnny
        - Joe
        - Josephine
        - Jim
        - Icarus

                            are all pieces of PIE

                (carefully selected, of course.)

If your parents object,

you say, "But Mom-Dad, you just don't understand that hang-gliding is a safe sport..."

That is your STATEMENT

Then

To get them to believe it so you can go on the weekend, too, you show them

- pictures & articles
  - in newspapers
  - in magazines
- a program on TV
- photos of Johnny & Josephine
  - taking off and landing

...all of which are pieces of PIE you have most carefully selected.

You note that you did not show them any items that indicated potential danger from such an activity...??

You use Pie this way; so do your friends, and your enemies, and your parents...

...and your Instructors and your textbooks,

because Pie makes people believe what you say or write.

The purpose and the effect of using PIE is

to guide, direct, or control
the mind of the reader or
the listener.

That is my   STATEMENT

.. Now let's see if I can
get you to believe it.

... I'll use a guy named "Oscar" as my   PIE

First I'll make a Statement about Oscar:

Oscar is a very good son.

If you look into your mind,
you will see that everything
is pretty clear except that...
your mind is wavering over the
meaning of "good"

Oscar is a very good son.

Now I give you a piece of Pie for
that Statement about Oscar:

21

- Whenever he robs a bank,
he gives half the take
to his mother.

Pie. And the mind snaps into focus on a
particular meaning of the word "good"

from the wavering

a   good   son

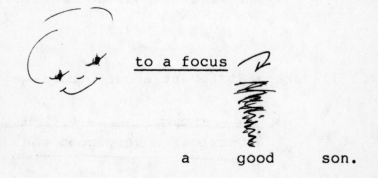

to a focus

a   good   son.

Now, still talking about the same
guy, I make another Statement:

Oscar is also a very good
husband.

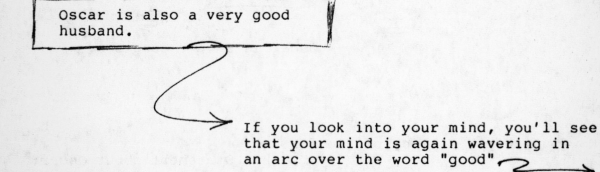

If you look into your mind, you'll see
that your mind is again wavering in
an arc over the word "good"

but  in as wide an arc this time:

first wavering

present wavering

Now I give PIE for the Statement that

Oscar is also a very good husband.

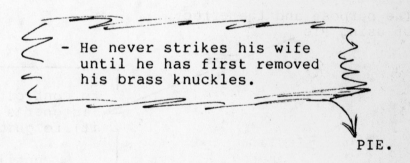

- He never strikes his wife
until he has first removed
his brass knuckles.

PIE.

And, again, what happens is...
the mind snaps into focus on a meaning of the word "good",

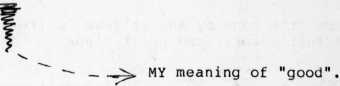

MY meaning of "good".

.. My meaning of "good" may seem
a peculiar meaning to you, but an idea
about Oscar...the kind of guy he is

is beginning to form in your head

because of the Pie you
have been fed about him.

Now I give you a third Statement about Oscar:

OSCAR IS A VERY GOOD FRIEND.

At this point some of you don't need any Pie about the kind
of GOOD FRIEND Oscar will be.

You wouldn't trust
him around the
corner.

The purpose and the effect
of using Pie   *is*

to control the reader or
listener's mind; to direct
it; to guide it

until it believes what
you have said in your
Statement.

That's how it's done by advertisers, writers of textbooks,
teachers/Instructors, and politicians

(and you)

(and me)

24

Up to here I have made two Statements:

(1) Everything, written or spoken, can be broken into two elements: Statement & Pie.

(2) The purpose of Pie is to guide, direct or control the mind of the reader or listener.

> At this point, you
> accept the second Statement
>
> because you were given Pie for it.
>
> You do not, and you
> should not, accept Statement number (1)
>
> because you were not given any Pie for it.

Let's have some Pie for St #1, and see what happens.

We'll use these subjects:

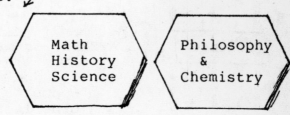

In Math a STATEMENT is made:

> "In order to maintain an equality, whatever you do to one side of an equation, you must also do to the other side of the equation."

PIE follows

- about 10 pages of proof, explanations (information) and examples.

25

In [History] a STATEMENT is made:

"There were three causes of this war."

PIE follows

- economic causes
- geographic causes
- political causes

Do you begin to recognize that you can also have Pie for economic causes???

You can, you know,
even though economic causes
is, itself, Pie for
"There were three causes..."

Explanation coming up soon.
Patience, please.

In [Science] a STATEMENT is made:

"Opposite electric charges attract each other with a force that varies in strength, depending on the distance between between the charges."

PIE follows

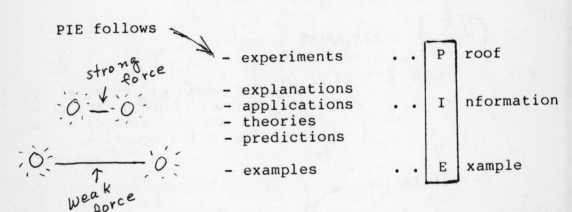

- experiments   . . P roof

- explanations
- applications   . . I nformation
- theories
- predictions

- examples   . . E xample

In ⌈ Philosophy ⌉ .. which can be messier than other subjects,

we will use two philosophers:

- Philosopher A ---- Ph. A
- Philosopher B ---- Ph. B

FIRST

Ph. A makes a STATEMENT: "God is dead."

Then she gives   PIE   to get you to believe her:

216 pages of a book which gives

- arguments
- explanations
- theories
- examples

THEN

Ph. B makes a STATEMENT: "Philosopher A is wrong."

And he gives   PIE   to get you to believe him:

429 pages of a book giving his

- proof
- information
- examples

THEN

Ph. A makes another STATEMENT:

"My learned friend, Philosopher B, is wrong."

and dishes out 1499 pages of Statements & Pies to get
you to believe her again.

which she calls "logic"

THEN

You guessed it.
Philosopher B gets into the act again.

And on and on it goes,
filling up all the shelves in the libraries.

But I think we'll tune out on them and ⟿

27

and switch to | Chemistry |

(St) → "Water changes its appearance as it goes from one
phase to another: from ice, to water, to steam."

(Pie) →   6 to 16 pages of

experiments
equations   proof/information

examples
structures
theory   information/example
reasons

Or perhaps you call all of these items "examples"?
It doesn't matter,

. your private language is your own,
. the name-tag you give an item is your free choice,
because
. the items are all just pieces of Pie.

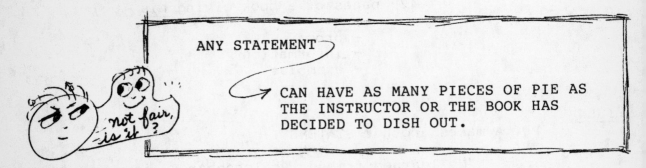

ANY STATEMENT

not fair,
is it?

CAN HAVE AS MANY PIECES OF PIE AS
THE INSTRUCTOR OR THE BOOK HAS
DECIDED TO DISH OUT.

A lot of Pie means a lot of detail.
Some people like things with a lot of detail,
some people don't.

But in this game you have to deal
with whatever comes down the road...

so let's look at

↳ what to do with the Pie

when you've got it.

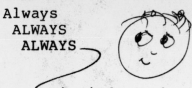

Always
ALWAYS
ALWAYS

indent the Pie under ITS OWN STATEMENT.

```
        - Statement A
            - Pie
            - Pie  >    for Statement A
            - Pie

        - Statement B
            - Pie
            - Pie  >    for Statement B
            - Pie
```

which gives you this kind of indented
pattern
for your notes

```
1 _____
  2 _____
  3 _____
  4 _____
5 _____
  6 _____
  7 _____
  8 _____
```

But, since you can have
Pie for Pie

(...patience,
explanation coming)

you can also have this kind
of pattern...

```
1 _____
  2 _____
  3 _____
      4 _____
      5 _____
  6 _____
    7 _____
      8 _____
      9 _____
```

which means that:

```
2, 3, 6 = Pie for 1        7 = Pie for 6
  4, 5 = Pie for 3      8, 9 = Pie for 7
```

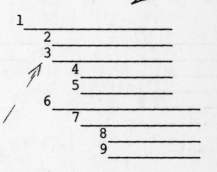

When you look at item 3

29

You can see that it is two things at once

.. it is Pie for Statement 1
.. it is Statement for items 4 & 5

When an item is both a Statement in the
material and a Pie, it has a double relationship.

This is very common, and is
one of the reasons you

must be sure to

keep all the Pie indents

lined up evenly with each other,

so you can know at a
glance which Pie belongs
to which Statement.

Let's say that ⟶ item 1 is the St   item 4 is Pie for 2
item 2 is Pie for 1   item 5 is Pie for 1
item 3 is Pie for 2   item 6 is Pie for 1

If you wrote it like this	If you wrote it like this	If you wrote it like this
1 _____ 2 _____ 3 _____ 4 _____ 5 _____ 6 _____	1 _____ 2 _____ 3 _____ 4 _____ 5 _____ 6 _____	1 _____ 2 _____ 3 _____ 4 _____ 5 _____ 6 _____
This is OKAY.	This is NOT okay.	This is NOT okay.
	Items 5 & 6 are not lined up with item 2. They are	Item 5 is not lined up with item 2. It is

Work. Yuck.

floating around in the notes,

unattached and useless.

30

Each piece of Pie
    must be indented correctly.
        Each piece belongs under its own Statement.

 Otherwise you get the information
                mixed up.

   (Usually people don't
                            get everything in its
                            correct spot at first.)

The problem is
that if you have incorrect
indents,

            you will have incorrect notes,
                which, when you memorize them for an exam,

                        will be a great waste of time.

Here is the kind of trouble you get into with incorrect
notes:

 | Oh, go away. |

Suppose you wrote these notes

- there are different types of cats
        - alphas
        - betas
        - caytas
        - raytas

            ...Then this is what you would write
                in an exam, or in a paper, or say
                to your Instructor:

                    "The four different types of
                    cats are the alphas, betas,
                    caytas and raytas."

...which is fine,
except that what the

Instructor had said, was

- there are different types of cats
  - alphas
  - betas
    - caytas
    - raytas

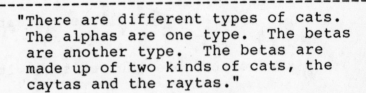

and what you were
supposed to come up
with is this

```
"There are different types of cats.
The alphas are one type.  The betas
are another type.  The betas are
made up of two kinds of cats, the
caytas and the raytas."
```

When this happens, there is
a loud complaint from a very
frustrated student,

"That's not what she said!
I can show you in my notes!"

Note taking is causing trouble!

However, the Instructor
should not be blamed
if your notes are
not correct.

```
            BOX FOR STUDENTS WHO WANT TO GET A's

There is a system for checking
whether your St-Pie indents are correct or not.


          You will find it on page 66.
```

Speakers and books sometimes give the Statement first, and the Pie last. Usually, however, they either dish it out in the opposite direction, giving Pie first and Statement last, because they like to lead up to their conclusion (which is really a Statement put at the bottom), or they use a "mixed" pattern, Pie-St-Pie, the reason being that they want to give background information as they talk/write, or they have mixed-up brains.

.. Now I'm going to St-Pie this for you.

- speakers and books
    - sometimes
        - give
            - St-Pie
    - usually
        - dish it out in opposite direction
            - Pie-St
            - reason = like to lead up to conclusion
                - concl. = Statement put at bottom
        (OR)
        - use "mixed" pattern
            - Pie-St-Pie
            - reason
                - want to give background info as talk/write
        (OR)
        - have mixed up brains

Because there are these
different language patterns,

the trick is to
take the stuff down
in your notebook,

<u>just as you hear it</u>...in whatever
St-Pie pattern it comes in.

And that night,

turn it all into the pattern
your mind likes best....

Why not? You're
the one who has
to learn it.

Look at these different St-Pie patterns.

In these paragraphs, the Statement is

"earliest great Western civilization".

WHAT WAS SAID	ST-PIE NOTES as you heard it

The earliest great Western civilization was that of ancient Greece and Rome. It lasted from 500 B.C. to 500 AD.	- earliest great West. civ.
	  - ancient Greece & Rome
	  - 500 BC - 500 AD
	
	St-Pie

500 B.C. to 500 A.D. was the period of ancient Greece and Rome, the time of the earliest great Western civilization.	- 500 BC - 500 AD
	  - ancient Greece & Rome
	  - earliest great West. civ
	
	Pie-St

The period of ancient Greece and Rome was the earliest great Western civilization, between 500 B.C. and 500 A.D.	- ancient Gr. & Rome period
	  - earliest great West. civ
	  - 500 BC - 500 AD
	
	Pie-St-Pie

ADVICE BOX

When you get these Pie-St or Pie-St-Pie patterns in your notes, as in the second and third versions above,

   - re-write them into a St-Pie pattern (using scratch paper)
   - & paste your re-write over the original notes.

      ...Or, if you prefer, you can paste it on the
         the page opposite your notes....This is part
         of the "Slot-in" technique, which will be
         explained in the next chapter.

         Patience. I can't do everything at once.

When you get stuff that you don't understand, in lecture or in books,

      start St-Pieing it anyway.

those are my relatives.

         As you work along, you begin to understand it,
         because St-Pie is a system for

            straightening out mixed up, difficult,
                  un-understandable stuff.

Here are some exercises for you
to practice on.

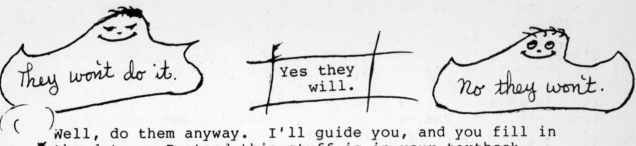

Well, do them anyway. I'll guide you, and you fill in
the dots....Pretend this stuff is in your textbook.

The population of the United States in 1980 was recorded
by the U.S. Census Bureau. There was a definite shift in the
population since 1970. The South and West were the fastest
growing areas, both in their numerical increase and in their
percentage increase. This shift in population is important
because the shift of population carries power with it:
political power because seats in the House of Representatives
are apportioned according to population, and financial power
because money from Federal Aid programs is often handed out on
the basis of population.

Population of U.S. (1980)
    - recorded by...............................
    - shift since 1970
        - South & West = fastest................
            - numerical.............................
            - percentage............................
    - important
        - carries...............................
            - political...........
                - seats in............................
                    - apportioned...................
            - financial............
                - money from......................
                    - often handed.....................

Exam questions you might have:

    Q.1 Did the South & West have a numerical or a percentage
                            \population increase?
    Q.2 What kind of power does a population shift carry with it?

Which would you rather study from at exam time: the textbook or
your St-Pie notes?

st-pie is extra work.

It is NOT. It's
LESS work if you have to
study for an exam.

Let's try this one. You fill in the dots.

The Personal Computer system is made up of several components. One of these components is the actual computer itself, the "brain", which includes the CPU (Central Processing Unit) and memory chips. The memory is made up of two different kinds of chips. The ROM (Read Only Memory) has information that is permanent; it cannot be changed or erased The RAM (Random Access Memory) has information that is transient. The RAM records the information and the instructions (the "programs") that you put in, but all of it disappears when the computer is turned off. However, another component, the storage device, while the computer is still on, stores the information and instructions for our later use. Cassettes and disks are two types of storage devices. Another component is the input device, examples of which are the keyboard (the most common), the joystick, the mouse, etc. Their purpose is the same, to put information and/or instructions into the computer. The fourth component is the output device. The two most commonly used are the monitor/video screen which lets us see what is going on, and the printer which gives us a permanent record.

Personal computer system = several components
  - the computer itself ("the brain") includes
      - CPU (Central..
      - memory......................
          - made of............................
              - ROM (Read.......................
                  - information = permanent
                  - cannot be.............................
              - RAM (Random.....................
                  - information = transient
                  - records what you put in
                      - information
                      - instructions (the................
                      - disappears when...............
  - the storage device
      - while computer.....................
          - stores............................
      - two types
          - ....
          - ....
  - the input device
      - examples
          - ...., ..., ..., etc.
      - purpose
          - ....
  - the output device
      - two most used
          - monitor/video = lets.......................
          - printer = gives.............................

Easier to study, huh?

36

CLUMPING...

                    is one of the neatest tricks in the game.

In your St-Pie notes,

> when you have words that mean
> about the same thing
>
> pick one of them as a Statement
> and Clump all the Pies under it.

Like this ⌐

```
---------------------------------------------------
| The apples we wanted were located in Jed's field. |
| They were a special kind of crab apple, and their |
| location was a spot that was hard to reach.       |
---------------------------------------------------
```

```
------------------------------------------
| ✓ - apples we wanted                     |
| ✓      - located                         |
| ✓          - in Jed's field              |
| ✓ - special kind of crab apple           |
| ✓ - location                             |
| ✓      - hard to reach                    |
------------------------------------------
```

LOCATED & LOCATION are words that have about the
same meaning.

          . Circle them.
          . Pick one as a Statement.
          . Clump the Pies under it.

                    And you get this ⇝→

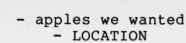

```
- apples we wanted              - apples we wanted
   - LOCATED                       - LOCATION
      - in Jed's field                - in Jed's field
      - hard to reach                 - hard to reach
   - special kind of crab apple    - special kind of crab
                                                      \apple
```

.. Choose one, copy it, paste it over your original notes.

ADVICE BOX

When you use an item from your original St-Pie notes,
which you do when Clumping or copying things,

      put a check-mark beside that item,

                  as I did.

Then, when you come back to your notes after
    you stopped for TV, conversation, food,
      whatever...

        your mind won't be skittering back and forth
          like a mouse, trying to decide, did I use
            this before? did I use that? did I
              put that down in two places ???

You won't have to go back
and waste time doing it over again.

Try St-Pie and Clumping on this one

   Scientific inquiry is an essential part of the
   function of the Universities. Science and education
   must be linked together in these schools of higher
   education. Universities have to be a bridge to the
   future. They cannot simply teach the past.

```
✓  - scientific inquiry
✓      - essential part of function of (Universities)
✓      - science & education
✓          - must be linked together in these (schls of higher
✓      - (Universities)                        \education)
✓          - must be bridge to future          ↳ my abbreviation
✓          - cannot simply teach the past
```

UNIVERSITIES & SCHOOLS OF HIGHER EDUCATION
have about the same meaning here.

                                    Circle them.
                                    Pick one as Statement.
                                    Clump the Pies under it.

                                            And you get ⟶

```
Universities
    - scientific inquiry = essential part of their fnc
    - must link together ⎰science
                         ⎱    &
                         ⎰ education        ↳ my
    - must be bridge to future               abbreviation
    - cannot simply teach the past
```

Now it flows right into your head, doesn't it?

            At exam time, you just have to glance at it.
            It will flow right back into your head again.

            You won't have to read it, examine it, and
            figure it out before you can memorize it.

                                    That's a promise.

Here's one to try on your own.
This one will have two
Statements to Clump under.

        they won't do it.   Yes, they will.   no, they won't.

39

Well, anyway, here it is.

```
- Taft-Hartley Act (1948)
    - made Labor Unions take additional responsibility
        - required 60 day cooling off period before action
                            \could be taken on issues
    - Management could get an injunction to require union
                            \workers to go back to work
                                \in case of a strike
    - prohibited Labor Unions from contributing to campaigns
                                \for office
    - employees could be spoken to directly by Management


        .Circle ⟨Labor Unions⟩ = Statement #1
        .Put a box around |Management| = Statement #2
        .Clump the Pies under their Statements
```

Did you get something like this?

```
-Taft-Hartley Act (1948)
    - Labor Unions
        - had to take additional responsibility
            - 60 day cooling off period required before action
                                \on issues
        - prohibited from contributing to campaigns for office
    - Management
        - could get injunction to require workers to go back to
                                \work in case of strike
        - could talk directly to employees
```

You did !! Great !!

> See? I told you so.   They don't
>   want to memorize
>   jumbled up stuff.

Clumping is an Information-Compactor.

    "Good" students use it all the time.

        It condenses your notes.
        It gets rid of repitition. And...you memorize
        bunches of the material while you are Clumping it.

Suppose you have a paragraph or a lecture
that goes like this ⌐

"As we know, there is a similarity between
the cytoplasm of animal cells and plant cell
cytoplasm."

```
· · · · · · · · · · · · · · · · · · · · · · · · · · · · · · · · · · ·
    - similarity between
        - cytoplasm of animal cells
        - plant cell cytoplasm
· · · · · · · · · · · · · · · · · · · · · · · · · · · · · · · · · · ·
```

Should we leave it like that?

It's okay, but it will be
easier to study at exam time,

if you line up words-that-are-repeated
under each other ⌐

```
· · · · · · · · · · · · · · · · · · · · · · · · · · · · · · · · · · ·
    - similarity between
        - plant   cell cytoplasm
        - animal  cell cytoplasm

(OR)
        - cytoplasm of plant  cells
        - cytoplasm of animal cells
· · · · · · · · · · · · · · · · · · · · · · · · · · · · · · · · · · ·
```

Here's another one with
repeat words you could line up ⌐

"Times change. Joshua, in the battle of Jericho, had
hundreds of men, but the men numbered in the tens of
thousands in the World War II South Pacific battle."

```
· · · · · · · · · · · · · · · · · · · · · · · · · · · · · · · · · · ·
                    - times change
  first             - Joshua
  notes                 - battle of Jericho
                        - hundreds of men
                    - men numbered in tens of thousands
                        - World War II
                        - S. Pacific battle
· · · · · · · · · · · · · · · · · · · · · · · · · · · · · · · · · · ·
```

```
................................................................
                    - times change
    St-Pie          - Joshua
    with                - battle of Jericho
    line-up             - men = hundreds
                    - World War II
                        - battle of S. Pacific
                        - men = tens of thousands
................................................................
```

Lining things up just makes it
easier to go over your notes
at exam time.

            And, of course, working over your notes
            this way, gets them partly memorized.

                                    Try it sometime.

Another line-up trick
you can use is putting
similar things under each other:

"The Zoo now had 300 animals. Giraffes counted
    for 52; 43 of the zebras were still there; birds
    up to 167 could be counted; and the remaining 38
    were a mix of many animals."

```
..................................................
                    - Zoo had 300 animals
    first           - giraffes = 52
    St-Pie          - 43 = zebras
    notes           - birds = 167

                    - 38 = mixed animals
..................................................
```

```
..................................................
                    - Zoo had 300 animals
    St-Pie          -  52 = giraffes
    with            -  43 = zebras
    line-up         - 167 = birds

                    -  38 = mixed animals
..................................................
```

It's fun.
            The mind likes order.
            It will memorize order.

    It won't memorize disorder.

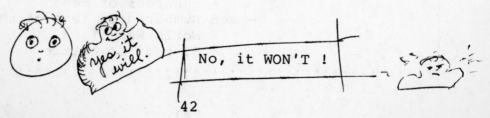

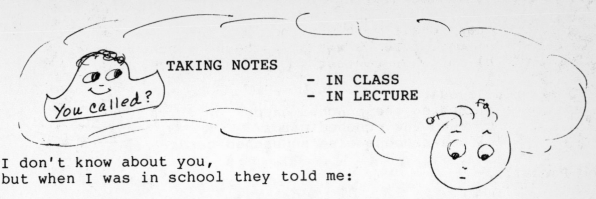

TAKING NOTES

- IN CLASS
- IN LECTURE

I don't know about you,
but when I was in school they told me:

Do NOT write down everything that the Instructor says.

Take down only the Important Ideas.
Take down only the Key Words.

I said how was I supposed to know what
the Important Ideas and Key Words
were when I didn't know the subject yet??

They said the Important Ideas were the
Big Picture, and the Key Words were the
Important ones, not all the little ones.

So, okay, I listened for a Big Picture idea,
and wrote down all the big words,
and left out the little ones.

This is the way my notes came out

. . . .
.   Calculating devices   .
.   Jacquard - dealt with weaving - used punched cards   .
.   Pascal - mechanical computer 1642   .
.   Babbage - analytical engine 1822   .
.   punched cards to control machine   .
.   John Von Newman - storing instructions (1943)   .
. . . .

ULCER FOOD !

A week later, I read them over for my exam.
They didn't make sense.

There wasn't any connection
between the big words. It sounded like
gibberish. It was gibberish.

I began to worry about answering the

exam questions.

43

Jacquard...what about him??

    Q 1: Jacquard dealt with weaving
             a) therefore he was able to use punched cards.
             b) in order to test the punched cards.

    Q 2: Did Jacquard
             a) design the punched cards?
             b) make the punched cards?
             c) use someone else's punched cards?

And Pascal...

    Q 3: Did Pascal
             a) design that mechanical computer he used?
             b) build that mechanical computer?
             c) use the University's mechanical computer?

And Babbage...

    Q 4: Was Babbage's analytical engine
             a) making punched cards to control another machine?
             b) controlled by Babbage's punched cards?

    Q 5: Did Babbage
             a) design the analytical engine?
             b) build the analytical engine?
             c) use someone else's analytical engine?

        (I don't even want to look at John Von Newman!)

I began to get the chills.
I stuck in all the little words
I could remember. It helped some, but
not enough. I couldn't remember enough about the lecture.

    I had to read the whole <u>textbook</u> on the topic.

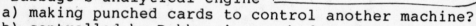

I complained about having to go over
the same material twice.

            They said if I had taken down
            the Important Ideas and Key Words
            I wouldn't need to do it twice.

I said how was I supposed to recognize
Important Ideas and Key Words when I
never even heard about the topic before??

            They said anyway it was good for
            me to be reading more widely
            on all subjects.

                                    Was I ever MAD!

44

I quit listening to them and
started to take down
EVERYTHING the Instructor said.

Here are some of the things I found out.

....

(1) When your Instructor is talking or lecturing:

   ..Take down EVERYTHING you possibly can.

   ..Try to keep the exact language of the Instructor.
                              \Do not try to paraphrase.

      If the Instructor says gluggle, you write gluggle.
      If the Instructor says sources of the conflict,

         you write sources of the conflict.

         Do NOT write ORIGINS of the conflict,
                  or CAUSES of the conflict.

   Changing the Instructor's language
            will get you into exam trouble,
                  which will be explained later in the book.)

(2) As your Instructor talks, there will be
      some parts that you hear in St-Pie form;

                  write them down that way,
                  & get the rest down any way you can.

(3) Sometimes your Instructors will say,
      "Don't take notes. Listen, so you
      will understand it."

                        TAKE NOTES.

←Never mind about relaxing. Your
                  Instructors just don't realize that
                  ORDINARY people, like us, understand
                  things five times better if we take
                  notes as we listen.

   Otherwise, we start daydreaming.

                  (Most school stuff isn't
                   exactly fascinating, you know.)

45

(4) If you don't understand
the material, take notes anyway.

You'll be surprised at how much
you will understand ⟩
↳ that night when you ⟩
←

(5) put it all into St-Pie form.

As you put your notes into St-Pie form,
you will recall a lot of things that
didn't get in. ⟩

. Add them in as you
make up your St-Pie units.

. Turn all the run-on sentences
and notes into St-Pie units.

. The first two weeks,

work, work, work!

there will be spots you can't
St-Pie. Put a question mark beside
them and ask a friend what they meant.

(6) Try this system in one course,
↳ for two weeks,
for half an hour a day.

When the two weeks is over,
there will be a large size bonus
waiting for you:

You will hear ALL your Instructors talking
more and more in St-Pie units,

because that IS how they talk.

You will have less and less fixing-up to do
on your notes at night,

because most of it gets done in class.

And, you will wonderfully understand what
is going on in your course.

Down with Homework

All of which is a pretty good
payload for half an hour a day,
for a couple of weeks,

↳ isn't it?

46

There are different things
that cause problems in lecture
note-taking.

. Sometimes
you don't have time to figure
out how to take down something
you don't understand.

. Other times you understand okay,
but don't know how to get it all down, like

You worry too much!

the Instructor is
talking <u>and</u> drawing on the
board at the same time.

. Or the thing that causes you
problems is the way the Instructor
jumps around from topic to topic.

The Instructor starts out talking
about animal G, and tells you
about its species,

then suddenly you're into the
habitats of animal K, and in two
sentences you're dumped into the
geological time period of animal Z,

followed by the courtship ritual of
animal G, the species of K, etc...

Now, there surely isn't time in
a lecture to take the notes
<u>and</u> solve the problems,

and you can't keep rushing back and forth
all over the page, trying to put the
animals together with their Pies.

But there's no need for all that hassle.

Lecture note-taking should be a quiet
and peaceful interlude in your day.

It should not be disrupted by
Things-That-Bother-You.

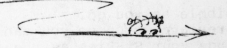

THING # 1

.. your notebook.

The best of the study game players use their notebooks for more than just taking notes. They use them to pull together

ALL the information from ALL their classes...lectures, texbooks and handouts.

THEY

. use a large size notebook, the loose-leaf type, so you can add & subtract pages,

. use only <u>one</u> side for the notes they take in class,

. leave the <u>other</u> side blank, to be filled in later with

      . Fix-ups of their lecture notes............. which you will learn how to do.

      . NEW information on the same subject, St-Pied from their textbooks and handouts............. which you will learn how to do.

      . Lab information, drawings & diagrams relating to the same subject.................. which you will learn how to do.

ADVICE BOX ON SCRIBBLE NOTES

Scribble as you go.
When you are St-Pieing material:→ textbooks, handouts, or your own run-on notes, use scratch paper, and

Scribble as you go.
Abbreviate words so you can work faster.
Change your St-Pies as the information becomes clearer.

Do Not Scribble.
It is BAD to scribble.

THING # 2

... the Fix-ups, which is your homework
    on your notes.

  ..Sometimes bits & pieces of your class or lecture notes
    don't come out in correct St-Pie indents.

    Some come out in run-on sentences;
    some are mixed-up St-Pies; and
        some are just bloopers you got wrong.

      ..These are all perfectly natural
        okay things to happen.

TO FIX THEM UP

  ..On the blank page opposite your lecture St-Pie notes,
    re-write these bits & pieces in correct St-Pie form.

    I use scratch paper for my St-Pie rewrites,
        and then I just paste it in on the
        opposite page.

  ..With colored pencil, draw a line through the incorrect
    notes,

    so that when you
    are ready to
    review for an
    exam, you won't
    be reviewing

    <u>incorrect</u>

    material.

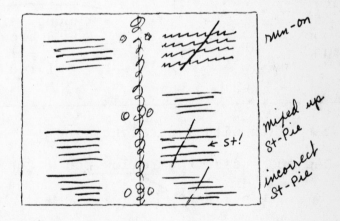

  ..You can get three wins out of these Fix-ups:

    ✓ - the bloopers in your notes get corrected,

    ✓ - you become skilled at St-Pieing anything, and

    ✓ - without any effort, you MEMORIZE one-third
        of the material.

                  Nice, huh ?

THING # 3

... is the Zilch, a trick to help you remember what your
notes meant. <u>Example</u>

. . . .
```
 The Instructor says                      You St-Pie

 "Red dog is the daughter of       - Red dog = dau of Yellow dog
  Yellow dog who had 4 pups,          - had 4 pups
  3 brown, one of which was              - 3 brown
  spotted, and one red."                     - 1 spotted
                                       - 1 red
```
. . . .

TODAY you can remember which dog had the pups.

>   But...three weeks and thirty pages of notes from now
>   you won't remember whether it was Red dog or Yellow dog
>   who had the pups, and you are then likely to come down
>   with the "what-did-I-mean" note-taking miseries.

To avoid the problem   _what problem?_   → use a Zilch.

```
                      |  - Red dog = dau. of Yellow dog
  margin              |
  of                  |   - 4 pups
  notebook            |      - 3 brown
  page                |           - 1 spotted        this
                      |      - 1 red                 is a
                      |                              Zilch
```

You can Zilch with a straight line   Or Zilch with an arrow

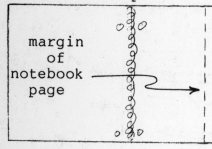

   - Red dog = dau.. of <u>Yellow dog</u>   - a package was in <u>the car</u>
                                                  - given by friends
              - 4 pups
                                              (gift from
                                                Aunt Joan)

A Zilch is used
   - to link items together
   - to Pie one part of a Statement
   - to give you freedom of the page in note-taking.

Anything { may be placed anywhere on the page,
          &
          Zilched into its proper St-Pie position.

THING # 4

... what do you do when you don't know where to put something?

Let's say the Instructor has been babbling along, and you've been St-Pieing & Zilching at a great rate. Suddenly the Instructor throws out a sentence that won't fit anywhere.

"The Red dog was the daughter of the Yellow dog who had 4 yellow and red pups. These are very common types."

You don't know which is the common type -- Red dog, Yellow dog, the pups, or all of them??

So you can't St-Pie it and you can't Zilch it.

But you can

put it AT THE MARGIN.

..And put a large question mark IN the margin, beside it.

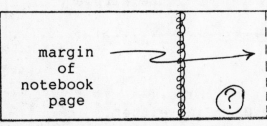

margin of notebook page	?	- Red dog = dau of Yellow dog - had 4 yellow & red pups They = very common types

The question mark is put in the margin
so YOU don't have to keep "remembering", for weeks or months,
that there was something you didn't understand, and what was it?

That evening, or next day, ask a friend who gets high grades which dogs the Instructor said was the "common type".

"Red dogs," says your friend.

"Aha!" says you, as you

Zilch the two items together, cross out or erase the question mark,

and smugly go off on a jogging spree, with your notes correct & ready for exam study.

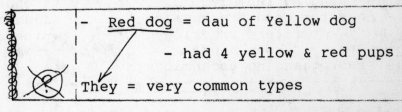

- Red dog = dau of Yellow dog
    - had 4 yellow & red pups
They = very common types

51

THING # 5

... what do you do when your Statements & Pies won't fit
onto one line of your notebook?

      (1) ... Begin the dash mark
           of your indents

              under the THIRD letter of the item
              above it....as I do in this book.

      (2) ... When you have extra stuff, put it on
           the next line
                  AT THE END of the line,
                  and use a SLANT mark...
                  as I do in this book.

Example

> "The manuals, supplied with the airplane kit, contain a great
> deal of information about the airplane, and are very useful."
>
>   - manuals
>   - supplied with airplane kit
>   - contain great deal of info about
>   \the airplane
>   - very useful

Here's another one with some
Pie that won't fit onto one
line....(I don't understand what the words mean, either. It
        doesn't matter. You can St-Pie it anyway.) Watch this

> "The command language provides a user interface to the
> process-handling and file-management facilities of the system."
>
>  - the command language
>   - provides a user interface to
>   - process-handling }
>   - file-management } facilities of
>   \the system

See?

EXAMPLE OF ST-PIE WITH & WITHOUT DASHES & SLANTS

TV is changing rapidly   TV is changing rapidly
- need for good programming   need for good programming
    \writers creating   writers creating new stuff
       \new stuff   fast changing technology
- fast changing technology

It's Not so bad!

THING # 6

> ... the Instructor jumps around from St-Pie to Pie-St to
> Pie-St-Pie and back again...how do you fix it in your notes?

. Take it down the way you hear it.
. Use Zilches & Margins as needed.
. That night, fix it up into St-Pie.

Examples:

(1) THE INSTRUCTOR SAYS

Helen is very rational.
Janet is emotional.
There is conflict between H & J.
Helen thinks reason brings change.
Janet thinks force brings change.

YOUR IN-CLASS NOTES	YOUR FIXED-UP NOTES

- Helen = very rational
- Janet = emotional
- conflict between H & J
- H thinks reason → change
- J thinks force → change
	- conflict betw. Helen & Janet
	  - Helen = very rational
	  - Janet = emotional
	  - ~~conflict between H & J~~
	  - H thinks reason → change
	  - J thinks force → change

The Fix-Up: Write in the St at the top.
Cross out, or erase, the St in the middle.

(2) THE INSTRUCTOR SAYS

Helen is very rational.
Janet is emotional.
Helen thinks reason brings change.
Janet thinks force brings change.
There is conflict between H & J.

YOUR IN-CLASS NOTES	YOUR FIXED-UP NOTES

- Helen = very rational
- Janet = emotional
- H thinks reason → change
- J thinks force → change
- conflict between H & J
	- conflict between Helen & Janet
	  - Helen = very rational
	  - Janet = emotional
	  - H thinks reason → change
	  - J thinks force → change
	  - ~~conflict between H & J~~

The Fix-Up: Write in the St at the top.
Cross out, or erase, the St at the bottom.

THING # 7

... what do you do with items that are connected by commas & and's...AND have the same Pie for all of them?

"Happiness comes from A, B, and C activities.

That's easy.

1) "List" the connected items

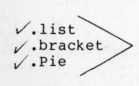

```
Your space
allowance
is used up!
```

```
- Happiness comes from

    - A..
    - B..
    - C..
```

2) "Bracket" the connected items

```
- Happiness comes from

    - A.. ⎫
    - B.. ⎬
    - C.. ⎭
```

3) Put the Pie ("activities")

<u>UNDER</u> THE BRACKETS   or   AT THE <u>SIDE</u> OF THE BRACKETS

```
- Happiness comes from

    -  ⎡ A..
    -  ⎢ B..
    -  ⎣ C..
            - activities
```

```
- Happiness comes from

    - A.. ⎫
    - B.. ⎬ activities
    - C.. ⎭
```

Try this one: "The new Personal Computers fulfilled the design and power requirements. They were impressive."

```
✓.list
✓.bracket
✓.Pie
```
>
```
- new Personal Computers
    - fulfilled
        - ⎡ design ⎤
        - ⎣ power  ⎦  requirements
    - impressive
```

You can use one-sided or both-sided brackets...
Whatever makes the information clear to you is fine.

THING # 8

... you go to the next page in your notebook -- where do you
start writing your notes?

You start ⟶ <u>at the margin</u> of the new page.

..Whether the item is a St or a Pie,
put it at the margin of the new page.

..If the item ⟋ is a piece of Pie, write
its Statement above it, in parenthesis.

<u>Like this</u>

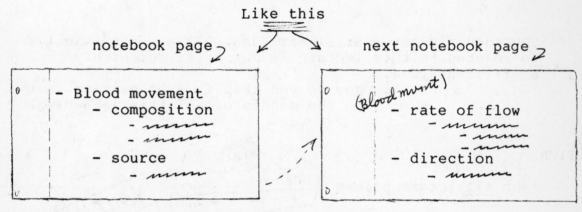

notebook page ⟍   next notebook page ⟍

If you do the margin/parenthesis,
whenever you see an item
in parentheses at the top of a page,

↳ you will know you are getting
a continuation from the preceding page,

and
⟹ you will know what the
Statement is for the Pies.

If you find yourself turning
the pages of your notebook
back and forth, trying to find out

what is talking about what,

you most surely do need to know
this game of easy note-taking.

THING # 9

... lecture interruptions.

1) The Instructor is babbling along and someone interrupts with a question.

> Where does the question and answer go?

2) The Instructor suddenly pauses, and then says, "Oh, by the way, I forgot to mention yesterday that the..."

> Where does yesterday's left-over go?

3) YOU suddenly get a Brilliant Idea. It may not exactly be related to this lecture -- but it is definitely a Brilliant Idea.

> How do you keep it from getting lost in the middle of all this jabbering?

SOLUTION

For <u>all</u> interruptions

- margin
- bracket } them
& - label

- continue with St-Pie as if they had not happened

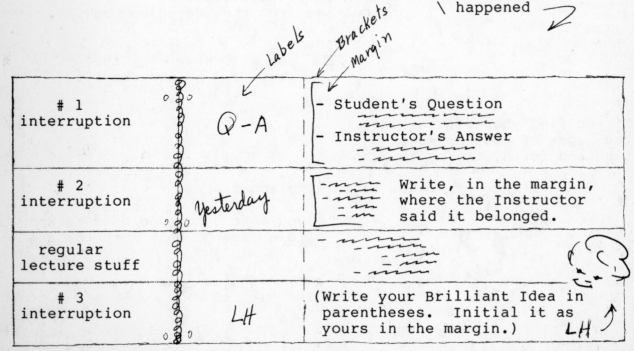

	Labels	Brackets / Margin
# 1 interruption	Q-A	[- Student's Question - Instructor's Answer
# 2 interruption	Yesterday	[Write, in the margin, where the Instructor said it belonged.
regular lecture stuff		
# 3 interruption	LH	(Write your Brilliant Idea in parentheses. Initial it as yours in the margin.) LH

THING # 10

>   ... what do you do when the Instructor writes something on
>   the board and talks about it at the same time?

WHAT YOU DO is

>   .. write down the NAME of the something that the
>   Instructor is writing on the board (the topic),

>   .. and St-Pie like mad everything the Instructor is
>   SAYING ABOUT it.

Example:

The Instructor says, "Now, then,
today we will be learning
about the various types
of numbers..." and slaps up
numbers all over the board.

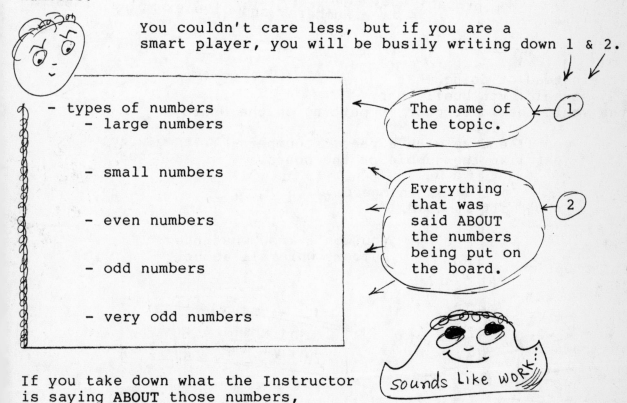

At the same time the Instructor talks about large numbers,
small ones, and even numbers, odd numbers and very odd
numbers.

You couldn't care less, but if you are a
smart player, you will be busily writing down 1 & 2.

- types of numbers
    - large numbers

    - small numbers

    - even numbers

    - odd numbers

    - very odd numbers

The name of
the topic.   ①

Everything
that was
said ABOUT
the numbers
being put on
the board.   ②

sounds like work

If you take down what the Instructor
is saying ABOUT those numbers,

>   you can get the numbers that the Instructor wrote on the
>   board later, from a friend or from a textbook.

>   Then you can fill in your notes, like this

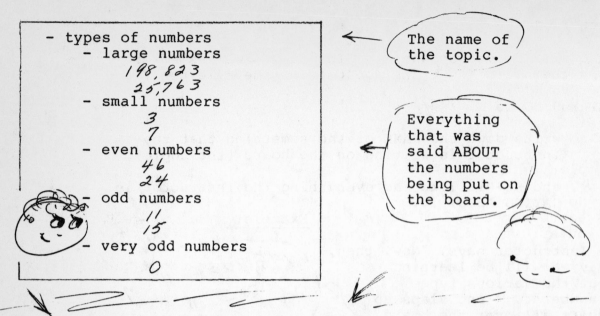

The exam question is NOT going to be: "What numbers did I put on the board last week?"

The exam question will probably be: "Name the different types of numbers, and give examples of each."

If, instead of doing what I just said, you busily copy the stuff the Instructor is putting on the board,

you'll end up with a page of numbers, just like the jumble on the board.

In 2 days, in one day, in half an hour,

you won't know what the numbers were all about.

... where do you write the Pie for a diagram that you <u>can</u> copy from the board during the lecture?

... That's easy ↱

put the Pie anywhere. Fix up the page that night.

<u>Example:</u> → The Instructor speaks ↱

"Now then, as you all know, a volcano is an opening in the earth's crust. The earth has four regions: the inner core, outer core, mantle and crust...."

↳ much drawing on the board while talking...

"...The chamber of the volcano, as you can see..."

↳ copy the drawing & scribble in the information ↱

"...lies above an area where pressure has caused a fracture in the crust and created a fissure. Molten matter from the interior of the earth forces its way through the fissure and erupts, finally, through the chamber of the volcano."

YOUR CLASS NOTES ↱

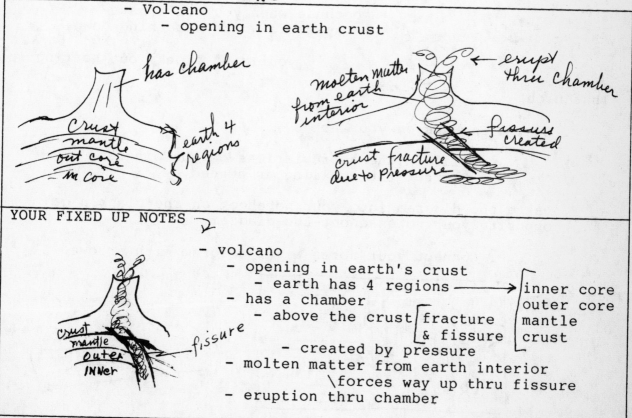

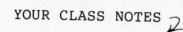

... what about diagrams that the Instructor hands out?

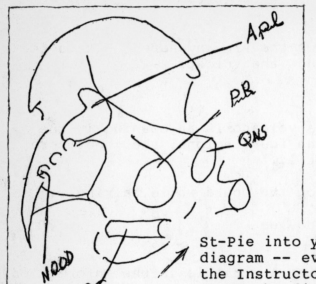

- LABEL the parts of the diagram on the handout as the Instructor speaks.

- ABBREVIATE. Use single letters or a few letters for the label. Write it out fully that night.

- Do NOT waste time on how to spell anything. You can look it up that night.

St-Pie into your notebook -- NOT onto the diagram -- everything the Instructor says ABOUT the diagram.

If you try to jam all the information onto the handout/diagram sheet

you will leave out a great deal that the Instructor says,

because when you don't have space to write something down,

your mind blocks out hearing it.

That night

. Do the Fix-ups on your notes.

. Fill in the abbreviations on the diagram.
. Correct the spelling as needed.

. Paste the diagram into your notebook on the blank page opposite your notes-about-the-diagram.

. Connect your notes & the diagram with arrows.

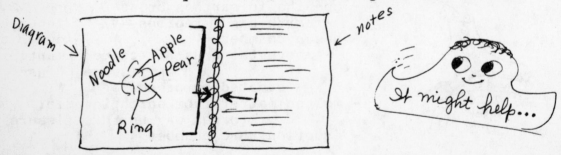

THING # 13

... your Instructors tell you to put things in your own
   words. To paraphrase. And I tell you not to.

   ? ????

I admit it's a problem.

   To get good grades you <u>have</u> to do what your
   Instructor says. There's no question about that.

   But, when you're taking notes,

      .in order to record the information correctly so
                        \you can <u>get</u> those good grades...
      you have to NOT do what the Instructor says.

                  (But don't go around talking about it.)

WHAT YOU DO is

   . St-Pie the material using the language of the Instructor
     or the textbook.

                  This allows you to get
                  the information down correctly.

```
....................................................
   "Ethnocentrism (Eth-no-cen-trism) is the human
    tendency to judge other cultures in terms of their
    similarity to our own culture."

      - Ethnocentrism
        - human tendency
          - to judge other cultures by similarity
                                      \to our own
....................................................
```

   . Now when you have to write it, or say it,
     to your Instructor,

                  USE A SERIES OF SHORT SENTENCES.

            It will come out sounding as if
            you "put it into your own words."

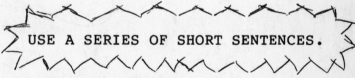

Sneaky, huh?

```
....................................................
   "Ethnocentrism is a human tendency.  It
    is a tendency to judge other cultures.
    We judge the other cultures by their
    similarity to our own culture.
....................................................
```

61

Here's another one to "put into your own words"
if you have to.

The Instructor/textbook has a Pie-St-Pie writing style.

```
.........................................................
  "It has been only in the last century that short stories as
  we know them have been written.  It was not until magazines
  became popular that these short stories began to appear.
  Since 1850 this new prose form, the short story, has
  become one of the most popular kinds of reading."

                    - short stories as we know them
                       - written only in the last century
St-Pie              - began to appear when magazines became popular
FIX-UP              - new prose form
                       - since 1850
                       - one of most popular kinds of reading
.........................................................
```

Use short
sentences
   to "put
   it in
your own
words".

```
.........................................................
  Short stories as we know them have been written
  only in the last century.  They began to appear
  when magazines became popular.  This new prose
  form, since 1850, is one of the most popular
  kinds of reading.
.........................................................
```

It's easy & it works &
I've been doing it this way for years.

If you have math or science courses

don't waste your time trying to paraphrase the stuff.

When you St-Pie it, you'll realize that
they've got practically every word fixed
so that

↳ each word means what it means,
and no other word means the same thing.

In this one ↘

> "Air enters the nose in two streams, because the nostrils
are separated by the septum. From the nostrils, air
enters the nasal passages which lie above the mouth cavity."

You can't paraphrase the passage into a tunnel. You can't
call the cavity a hole, or the septum a bone....And you sure
as the sun rises can't change how the air travels in the body!

So just St-Pie it, and let it be.

If you have to "put it in your own words"

It absolutely works.
I promise.

⤷ use the series of short sentences.

St-Pie ↘

air
- enters nose in 2 streams
  - reason
    - nostrils separated
      \by septum
- from nostrils
  - enters nasal passages

↙ lie above mouth
\cavity

Your own words ↘

Air enters the nose in
two streams. There is a
reason for this. The
nostrils are separated
by the septum. From the
nostrils the air enters
the nasal passages.
These passages lie above
the mouth cavity.

For me, the easiest way to learn
this kind of tightly written
material

is to make a sketch
as I read it.

Try it.   Like this ➡

63

THING # 14

... rhetorical questions.

That's when your Instructors ask questions they intend
to answer themselves.

You are not supposed to raise your hand and
answer a rhetorical question.

Example: Your Instructor says, "Now then, what
is it, exactly, that a cell does?"

What you are supposed to do is

. Turn the rhetorical question
into a Statement as best you can.

Sometimes you can do it in class; if not,
you can do it at night in your Fix-ups.

. Then St-Pie the information under it.

Rhetorical Q # 1... "Now then, what is it exactly that
a cell does?"

Turn the question into a Statement.
Then add the Pie.

- what a cell does   OR   - cell functions
  - multiplies   - multiplies
  - transforms   - transforms
     \energy   \energy
....

Rhetorical Q # 2... "Why, then, do apples fall to the ground?"

Turn the question into a Statement.
Then add the Pie.

- apples fall to ground
  - reason
    - gravity
    - no equal opposing force

THING # 15

... abbreviations.

. They are wonderfully useful things.
  They help you get down everything that's being said.

   In lecture or in class, never bother with
   spelling...only with getting the information.

      Fix-up the spelling at night.

   Make up your abbreviations at night, when
   you're doing the Fix-ups.

 Experiment.

↳ .. For example, which of these do you like?

- function	fnc	func
- reaction	rxn	reac
- example	ex	e.g.
- system	sys	syst
- national	nat	nat'l
- location	loc	loca

and how about ⤳ w/   for "with"
                  w/o   for "without"
                  @   for "approximately" or "about" ??

Do you know about abbreviating by
leaving out most of the vowels in words?

gvnmnt	...	for government
txtbks	...	for textbooks
mthd	...	for method
hstry	...	for history
scnc	...	for science

(Some people call this Speed-Writing.)

   That night, in the Fix-ups,
   write out the ones
   you aren't sure about,

      like "mthd" & "scnc".

...IF you want to check your notes:

     For example, if you've made notes to write
          a paper,
              or you want to be sure your
              notes are correct for an exam,

...you can use the Sentence Check Out (SCO) system.

   . You read down your page of notes,
    making sentences out of the Statement and
    each of its Pies.

       - If the sentence gives you incorrect
        information, something is wrong.

       - If the St-Pie doesn't make a sensible
        sentence, something is wrong.

Example: your notes

- different types of cats
  - alpha
  - beta
  - cayta
    - rayta

To check them out,
  read them into sentences

Alpha is one of the different types of cats.

Beta is one of the different types of cats.

Cayta is one of the different types of cats -- WHOA!
that's not right! The Instructor said a cayta was a
TYPE OF BETA...okay, proceed...

A rayta is a type of cayta. No, that's not right....
A cayta is a rayta? Huh? That's nonsense....

    A rayta is <u>also</u> a type of beta cats...whew! I
    better indent caytas & raytas under betas...."

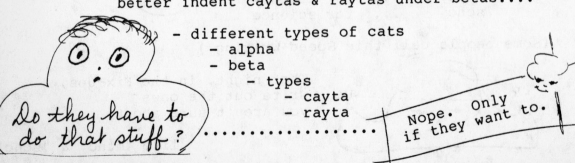

    - different types of cats
      - alpha
      - beta
        - types
          - cayta
          - rayta

Do they have to do that stuff?

Nope. Only if they want to.

... the Slot-ins, which pull everything together for you

        → when you get lectures AND textbook
          or laboratory assignments on the same
          topic...and, probably, your Instructor
          also gives you some handouts.

THE PROCEDURE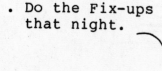

. St-Pie the lecture. Get down everything you can.

. Do the Fix-ups
  that night.

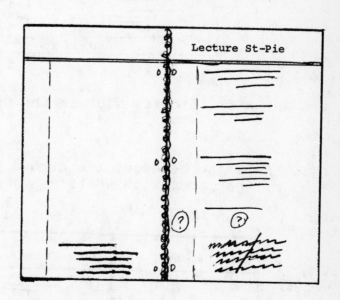

Lecture St-Pie

. Now

    ..... Skim your lab sheets, textbook or handouts for any
          NEW information that you didn't get in the lecture.

              → Ignore everything in the lab sheets,
          textbook or handout that is already in your
          notes.

    ..... On the blank page opposite your St-Pie
          notes, write in (or paste in) your St-Pie
          of this NEW information. ──────────→

That's all kid stuff.

67

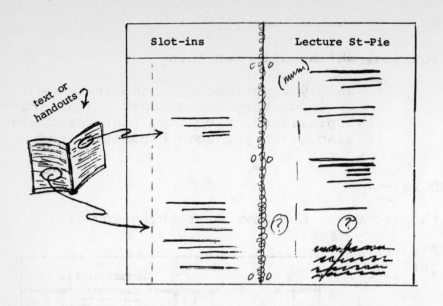

text or
handouts

... and ARROW IT into its slot in the St-Pie lecture notes.

... Make the heads of the arrows MEET, so you know
what goes with what,

like this

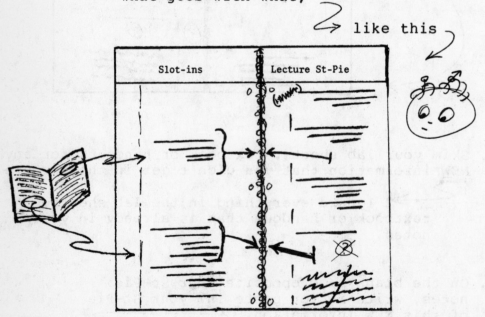

If you need more space for a particular notebook page,

✓ tape more paper to the Slot-in page, and
✓ fold this extra paper into the notebook.

Now, everything -- from your lectures, texbooks,
labs and handouts

is altogether in one place
without any repetitions in the material.

At exam time, you can leave your
handouts in their pile, and your
textbooks on their shelves, and
study from your single notebook.

It makes you feel
frightfully superior.

AND very tiRED?

It's not THAT
much work !!

When you study this way, you don't get tired.
You don't get bored. And
your mind keeps on memorizing
whole globs of the material.

WHEN YOU DON'T HAVE REGULAR LECTURES

. St-Pie what your Instructor says in the class.
. Do the Fix-ups.

Instructors give their clues for the
exam questions in lecture and in class.

To be explained in the next chapter.

EXPLANATION BOX ABOUT SKIMMING

..It is a very pleasant feeling,
  when you are skimming textbooks and handouts
  to find that you are going at a very fast rate.

This happens because after you have done the Fix-ups,
you have lecture or class notes

↳ that are correct, easy to read,
   one-third memorized, and clear in your mind.

..When anything is clear in your mind, and you are
  skimming material on that same subject,

↳ your mind moves swiftly past what it already understands.

THING # 18

... how do you keep your notes looking neat if you are Zilching, Fixing-up notes, Slotting-in stuff, and putting in arrows all over the page?

ANSWER

Do not waste your time on such nonsense.

Neatness is completely unimportant.

No one sees your notes but you and God, and
     God is too busy to bother with such trivia.

You are no longer in elementary school.

Get down what the Instructor says and get it
     down correctly.

It is no comfort to be called "The neatest C minus
     in the class."

The only thing of importance to anyone is your performance.
You get no points for "effort" now.

                 This is the outside world...

4

HOW TO FIND THE EXAM QUESTIONS

Most people, even a few geniuses,
are interested in figuring out

> ahead of time what the exam questions
> are going to be.

So, what we'll do next is learn
the part of the study game that

> shows you how to find the
> exam questions.

You already know
the Instructor talks
in St-Pie

> even though he
> doesn't know
> what he's doing.

Here is the Instructor

And you can take
good notes in
St-Pie

> so what HE said,
> YOU got down during
> the lecture.

Here is the Student

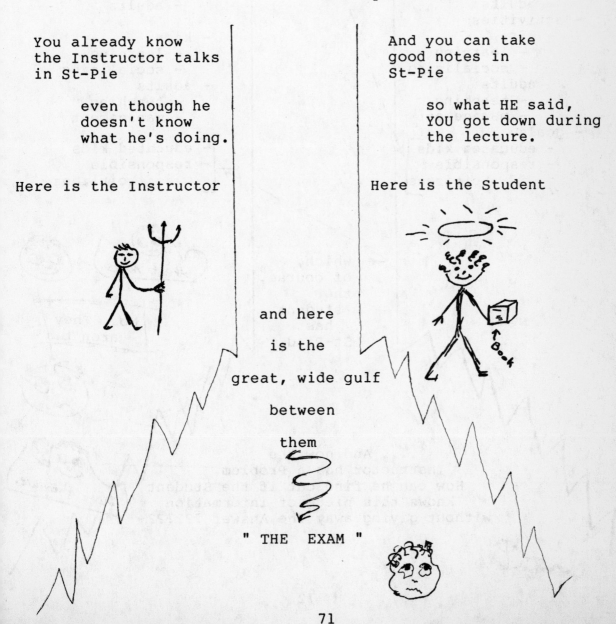

and here

is the

great, wide gulf

between

them

" THE EXAM "

The Instructor has lectured.
The Student has taken notes.

The Instructor now has to make up the Exam Questions. He
wants to know if the Student knows this pair of items
that he taught...

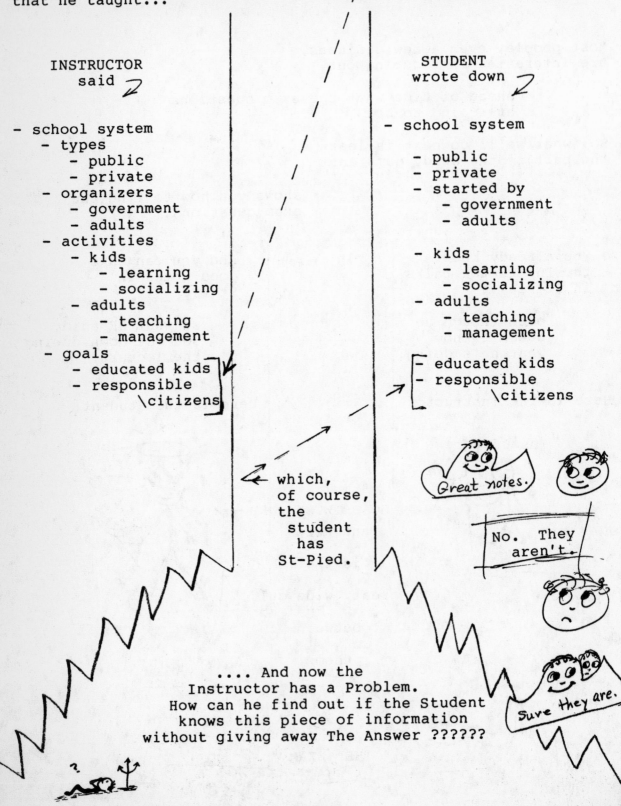

INSTRUCTOR
  said

- school system
  - types
    - public
    - private
  - organizers
    - government
    - adults
  - activities
    - kids
      - learning
      - socializing
    - adults
      - teaching
      - management
  - goals
    - educated kids
    - responsible
        \citizens

STUDENT
wrote down

- school system
    - public
    - private
    - started by
      - government
      - adults

  - kids
    - learning
    - socializing
  - adults
    - teaching
    - management

  - educated kids
  - responsible
      \citizens

which,
of course,
the
student
has
St-Pied.

Great notes.

No. They
aren't.

Sure they are.

.... And now the
Instructor has a Problem.
How can he find out if the Student
knows this piece of information
without giving away The Answer ??????

When an Instructor has a Problem, he begins to talk to himself like this: "Now, let me see. This stuff is actually talking about the goals of the school system. / So..."

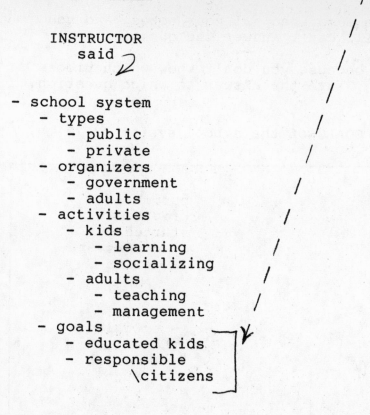

INSTRUCTOR
said

- school system
  - types
    - public
    - private
  - organizers
    - government
    - adults
  - activities
    - kids
      - learning
      - socializing
    - adults
      - teaching
      - management
  - goals
    - educated kids
    - responsible
          \citizens

So the Instructor uses   GOALS   as the

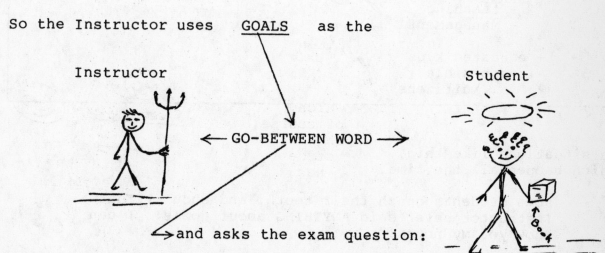

Instructor   Student

← GO-BETWEEN WORD →

→ and asks the exam question:

What are the GOALS of the school system?

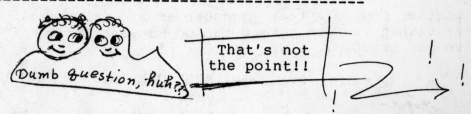

Dumb question, huh??

That's not
the point!!

73

IF YOU DO NOT KNOW THE
GO-BETWEEN WORD, YOU'VE
GOT TROUBLE.

You've memorized all your notes, and you
still can't answer the question

because you don't know which pieces
are the answer to which question.

What are the GOALS of the school system ?????

Your notes

- school system

    - public
    - private
    - started by
        - government
        - adults

    - kids
        - learning
        - socializing
    - adults
        - teaching
        - management

    - educated kids
    - responsible
            \citizens

goal?
goal?
goal?

In situations like this,
which happen all the time,

some students gnash their teeth, and shout, "That
Instructor never said ANYTHING about goals! I can
show you my notes!"

Other students just wilt,
and feel sad.

But whether you're a teeth gnasher or a
wilter...when you don't know the Go-Between Words,
you've got trouble.

AND MORE TROUBLE COMING

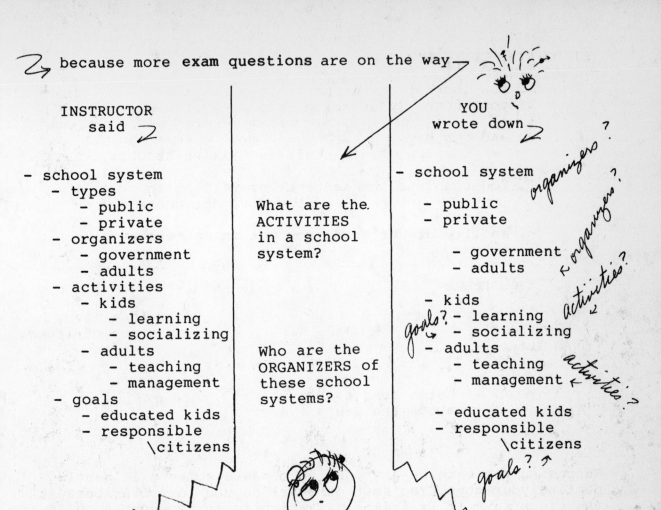

because more **exam questions are on the way**

INSTRUCTOR
said

YOU
wrote down

- school system
  - types
    - public
    - private
  - organizers
    - government
    - adults
  - activities
    - kids
      - learning
      - socializing
    - adults
      - teaching
      - management
- goals
  - educated kids
  - responsible
    \citizens

What are the
ACTIVITIES
in a school
system?

Who are the
ORGANIZERS of
these school
systems?

- school system
  - public
  - private
    - government
    - adults
    - kids
    - learning   *organizers?* *organizers?* *← organizers* *activities?* *goals?*
    - socializing
  - adults
    - teaching
    - management   *← activities?*
  - educated kids
  - responsible
    \citizens
    goals? ↗

Yikes!!! There must be an easier way to live...I think???

Sure there is.

<u>First:</u> you find the G-B's (the Go-Betweens).

<u>Second:</u> you use them to figure out the
exam questions.

Both are easy as Pie to do.

Well...if it's easy.

Let's do them in order ⟶

(1) TO FIND THE G-B's

. You look at any item or group of items in
  your notes, your textbooks, or your handouts

. and you say,
                    "This stuff is talking about..........."

. You complete the sentence by filling in
                    the dot, dot, dots

. and...whatever words you put in up here

IS THE G-B

for that item,
or group of items.

Let's read a story
about the G-B's

Supposing you wake up one morning because someone is gently
patting your toes. You sort of snarl as you turn over because
the clock says it is 4:46 a.m., which is an indecent hour in
your life. However, when you see the gentle creature which is
gently patting your toes, you stop snarling. You find
yourself suddenly sitting up with your mouth hanging open and
your hands clutching the blanket that's got itself twisted
around your underarm and neck.

The gentle creature stops gently patting your toes as it sees
you are awake. It moves backward one step, and speaks to you.

"I am happy to know you," it says with a certain formality of
voice. "I am a visitor from a planet in the Horsehead Nebula.
That is an area in Space. I have been instructed that
communication can be accomplished between us by describing
myself using Statement-Pies and Go-Betweens, which I will now
do.

"My hair is a radiant green, and ← *items*
I have three eyes -- two in front
and one behind my head. The color
of my eyes is pale purple. My
nose and my mouth are somewhat as   All of this
the human one, but smaller, and   stuff is talking about
my skin is a glowing blue.   my appearance.
                                      ....

76

"I am kind and gentle to everyone and thing. I am modest and
curious about all ones and
things in the Universe.

"I hate playing UFO, and do not
like my Beyond-The-Nebula Planet
School for teaching it to us.

"My greatest talent is in
rhythmic antennae-twitching.
I have won many star globes
for my displays.

←*items*

All of this
stuff is talking about
my personality.
· · · · · · · · · · · · ·

All of this
stuff is talking about
my dislikes.
· · · · · · · · · ·

←G-B's

All of this
stuff is talking about
my talents.
· · · · · · · · · ·

"I communicate in this way through the use of Statement-Pies
and the Go-Betweens, since all intelligent life forms are
known to be able to use either or both. The more intelligent
can use both, and I request knowledge of which you use."

It is to be hoped that at this
point you will close your mouth,
stop clutching your blanket, and
say in a casual tone, "Both. Naturally."

Having now lied to save the honor of the human race,
let's do some work with the G-B's

so you can keep up with the visitor from
the Horsehead Nebula.

WHENEVER YOU

FIND A G-B for an item, or group of items

    .. if you hear one in a lecture,
    .. if you recognize one in a textbook
                  \or a handout,
    .. if you figure one out during the Fix-ups,

WRITE IT IN AS A STATEMENT for that item, or group of items.

       Let's try it on the visitor from the Horsehead Nebula.

St-Pie of items 2	G-B's put in as Statements for the items 2
--------	----------

- hair
   - radiant green
- eyes
   - pale purple color
   - 2 in front
   - 1 behind
- ⎡nose &
  ⎣mouth
     - sm./humanlike
- skin = glowing blue
 	
- kind & gentle
   - to ⎡everyone
       ⎣everything
- modest
- curious about
   - all ⎡people &
       ⎣things
 	
- hates playing UFO
- dislikes school for
    \teaching UFO
- TALENT
   - rhythmic anten.
     \twitching
   - won star globes
	- APPEARANCE
	  - hair
	    - radiant green
	  - eyes
	    - pale purple color
	    - 2 in front
	    - 1 behind
	  - ⎡nose &
	   ⎣mouth
	      - sm./humanlike
	  - skin = glowing blue
	- PERSONALITY
	  - kind & gentle
	    - to ⎡everyone
	        ⎣everything
	  - modest
	  - curious about
	    - all ⎡people &
	        ⎣things
	- DISLIKES
	  - playing UFO
	  - school for teaching UFO
	- TALENT
	  - rhythmic anten. twitching
	    - won star globes

group of items (handwritten)

single item (handwritten)

A G-B which you heard as
you were taking notes.

    .. How would you like to
       study for an exam from these   notes?

                                    Neat, huh?

(2) TO FIND THE EXAM QUESTIONS FOR ANY MATERIAL,

    . you first write in the G-B's as Statements, which we just did,

    . then

YOU MAKE UP A QUESTION USING A G-B.

That's the exam question.

The answer to that question is the St-Pie under that G-B.

Let's practice on the visitor from the Horsehead Nebula again.

We'll write the question for each G-B in several ways.

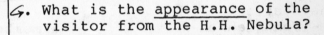

Notes with G-B's ↗	Exam Questions ↗

- APPEARANCE
  - hair
    - radiant green
  - eyes
    - pale purple color
    - 2 in front
    - 1 behind
  - ⌈nose &
    ⌊mouth
     - sm. humanlike
  - skin = glowing blue
	G. What is the <u>appearance</u> of the visitor from the H.H. Nebula?
	
	  . Describe the <u>appearance</u> of the visitor from the H.H.Neb.
	
	    . Why was the <u>appearance</u> of the visitor unusual?

- PERSONALITY
  - kind & gentle
    - to ⌈everyone
       ⌊everything
  - modest
  - curious about
    - all ⌈people &
       ⌊things
	G. What kind of <u>personality</u> did the visitor think he had?
	
	  . Describe the visitor's idea of his <u>personality</u>.

- DISLIKES
  - playing UFO
  - school for tchng UFO
	G. Describe the visitor's <u>dislikes</u>.
	  . Why did the visitor <u>dislike</u> \his school?

- TALENT
  - rhythmic anten.
    \twitching
    - won star globes
	. What was the visitor's <u>talent</u>?
	  . What did his <u>talent</u> win him?

THE ANSWER to any of these Exam Questions ↘

    IS THE ST-PIE INFORMATION
    UNDER THE G-B.

Sneaky, huh?

SOMETIMES the Instructor asks the exam question backwards

using the Pie to make up the question.

When this happens,
the Pie is the question,
& the G-B is the answer.

The St-Pies and the G-B's
go back and forth as
questions and answers
for each other.

Let's see
how it works.

```
....................................................................
: Here are the St-Pie notes    :        Here are the G-B's          :
:                              :                                    :
:                              :      (THIS STUFF)    IS TALKING ABOUT :
:                              :                                    :
: - The Beatles                :                                    :
:    - John Lennon             :   a member                         :
:    - Paul McCartney          :   a member                         :
:    - Liverpool               :   where they started               :
:    - The Yellow Submarine    :   one of their songs               :
....................................................................
```

WRITE IN THE G-B's
as Statements

Here are the BACKWARDS EXAM
QUESTIONS, using the Pie

```
....................................................................
: - The Beatles                :                                    :
:    - 2 of the members        :  ..Who are Lennon & McCartney?      :
:       - John Lennon          :                                    :
:       - Paul McCartney       :                                    :
:                              :                                    :
:    - where they started      :  ..What is Liverpool famous for?    :
:       - Liverpool            :                                    :
:                              :                                    :
:    - one of their songs      :  ..Identify "The Yellow Submarine". :
:       - The Yel. Sub.        :                                    :
....................................................................
```

SAD STORY

Once there was a sad student who became a happy
student. She read up to here in this book, and
lights began to go on in her head.
"Of course!" she exclaimed. "Of
course! Naturally! Of course!"

(Sad Story continued on next page)

She smiled in school as she walked from class to class; she smiled at home as she read her textbooks; and she nodded her head in understanding as the Instructors talked, because each one was sending out a steady stream of St-Pies and G-B's.

She smiled at the exam on her desk, and she smiled happily as she wrote out the answers and filled in the blanks. Exams were beginning to be NOT HORRIBLE!

And then, one day, she stopped smiling. The Instructor handed back the exams. Her grade was very low. It was horrible. Exams were horrible. Instructors were horrible. What had gone wrong?

The student had understood all the St-Pie and Go-Between theory so easily,

and it had made so much sense, and it had seemed so natural,

that she didn't think she needed to actually take notes, or do the Fix-ups, or write in the G-B's....

They can't do EVERYTHING

But she was wrong.

You do have to.

You want them to get rotten grades??!??

In the exam, it had been easy to answer the questions, because she remembered a LOT of St-Pies.

But some of the ones she remembered were not correct, because she hadn't done any Fix-ups.

And with all the G-B's not written down, and just floating loose in her head from the weeks of classes

a bunch of the G-B's had attached themselves to the wrong St-Pies in her memory. So she answered the G-B questions with the wrong St-Pies.

So she got a poor grade.

It really is a sad story.

When you're after easy, good grades
you have to Fix-up your notes

⤷ and you have to add in the INSTRUCTOR's G-B's.

It doesn't do any good
to put into your notes

the G-B's you made up for yourself,
or found in a textbook,
or got from another Instructor.

Aw, come on

The G-B's that YOUR
Instructor used in your class

are the ones your Instructor
intends to use to make up your exam questions.

That's a fact of life.

And if you don't know your
Instructor's G-B's for the
different parts of the notes ⟶ you've got ⟶ trouble.

If the Instructor called column A the "GOVERNMENT ORGANIZATION"

and you thought of it as the "POLITICAL ORGANIZATION"

and the Instructor said columns B & C were

talking about | POLITICAL ORGANIZATION
                &
              AGREEMENTS

but you wrote down
that columns B & C were ⤵ GOVERNMENT ORGANIZATION & RESULTS

Like this ⟶

	column A	column B	column C
Instr. G-B's	government organization	political organization	agreements
Your G-B's	political organization	government organization	results

82

Then you may be on an
asphalt Freeway to Exam Troubles.

Because this ⤳ is what ⤳ has happened ⤳

```
the Instructor said                        you wrote down
  ------                                      ------

   Country X              Instructor          Country X
     - gov't organiz.       G-B's    ←          - polit. organiz.
        - abc                                      - abc
     - polit. organiz.                          - gov't organiz.
        - def              Your                    - def
     - agreements          G-B's    →           - results
        - ghi                                      - ghi
```

and
the exam questions

Q.1   Describe the government organization
      in Country X.

Q.2   What was the political organization
      in Country X?

Q.3   Which agreement was most important
      to Country X?

   ??...??...? %#$@?!!%&*$#??...He never
even MENTIONED agreements....$?%&#@?"%!+??!!!

And the result

	Instructor answer	Your answer	Your credit
Q. 1	abc	def	zero
Q. 2	def	abc	zero
Q. 3	ghi	?!???	zero

I don't blame you. It's enough to upset an angel.

So next time don't "study" so much, and spend 15 minutes a night on each lecture adding the Instructor's Go-Betweens into your St-Pie notes.

You do understand, don't you, that Instructors don't particularly <u>want</u> to give you the exam question G-B's?

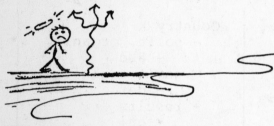

It's just one of the things they can't help. The G-B's come out everywhere as they talk.

The most important times for hearing their G-B's are

. at the BEGINNING of the class,
. at the END of the class,

To get them into your notes you need to do two things:

---

*   ALWAYS TAKE DOWN and ST-PIE
    EVERYTHING THE INSTRUCTOR SAYS

        IN THE <u>FIRST FIVE MINUTES</u> OF CLASS.

                ..Your Instructor may be
                reviewing yesterday's lecture
                    ..or previewing today's lecture.

                ..Review or Preview, it will have
                the exam question G-B's in it.

*   ALWAYS TAKE DOWN and ST-PIE
    EVERYTHING THE INSTRUCTOR SAYS

        IN THE <u>LAST FIVE MINUTES</u> OF CLASS.

                ..Your Instructor may be
                summarizing today's lecture,
                    ..or previewing tomorrow's.

                ..Summary or Preview, it will have
                the exam question G-B's in it.

Let's play school.

Pretend today is Monday. You are in class and, before you are
barely seated, the Instructor has started babbling away. In
practically a panic, you yank out a pen and slam open your
notebook to any clean page.

"...in the next lectures," says your Instructor, "we
will look at the Rock 'n Roll Cycle. The Cycle will
be discussed in terms of its functions in society and
the changes that occur within the Cycle. We will, in
addition, examine the reactions of people to the Cycle,
and the mechanisms that create these reactions.

Oh yuck. Who cares?

You do.
You are scribbling in your notebook
like all the demons of Hell are
after you

even though you never heard of a Rock 'n Roll
Cycle, and don't know what a mechanism is or
isn't...into your notebook goes everything!

```
- Rock 'n Roll Cycle
    - functions in society
    - changes within it
    - rxns of people to it
        - mechs that create rxns
```

"...now this Cycle," says the Instructor...and you get a
chance to wiggle out of your jacket, take a breath, and settle
in to take notes on the lecture in a relaxed, easy fashion.

The day flows happily or miserably along from class to class
and friend to friend, with a sandwich here and a cookie there,
until now it is nighttime. You are at home and the time has
come. You sigh, place your notebook on your desk, light the
lamp, sigh again, and...face the Fix-ups & adding in the G-B's.

Well !! Look at that!
Your St-Pie notes are
pretty o.k. Well.
How do you like that?
Not bad, not bad, huh?

Well, ok, ok. Now where's the stuff from the beginning of class?? That'll give me the G-B's

fnc..change..rxn..mech..??

Yeah. Probably...

. . . .

Your class notes   G-B's

This stuff   is talking about   G-B's added in

Rock 'n Roll Cycle

_____
_____
_____

_____
_____

_____
_____

_____

_____

_____

_____

_____
_____

_____

the FUNCTIONS IN
SOCIETY of Cycle.

Fnc in soc = G-B

the CHANGES
within the Cycle.

Changes = G-B

the REACTIONS
OF PEOPLE to
Cycle.

Rxns of ple = G-B

the MECHANISMS of
THE CYCLE.

Mech of cycl= G-B

Rock 'n Roll Cycle
  - functions in soc (3)

_____
_____

  - changes within it (3)

_____
_____
_____

_____
_____

  - rxns of people (2)

_____

_____
_____

_____

  ──→ - Mechs........

_____

_____

Nope. Wrong. ─ ─

 They're talking about the
MECHANISMS THAT CREATE THE REACTIONS.

OK, then these mechanisms are
Pie for the "REACTIONS" G-B.

Well. That wasn't so bad...

Bad enough! Work!

steam from
over-heating
of brain.

Okay, let's see what
the exam questions will be.

1) What FUNCTIONS are served by the Rock 'n Roll Cycle?

        (Not bad..there are three of them.)

2) What CHANGES occur within the R-n-R Cycle? Describe one.

        (Easy. Two of them. I'll describe b.)

3) In what order do the REACTIONS OF PEOPLE to the R-n-R Cycle
                        \take place?
        (x first, then y.)

4) In the R-n-R Cycle, are the two MECHANISMS

        (a) mechanisms of the Cycle?
        (b) mechanisms of peoples' reactions to the Cycle?
        (c) mechanisms that create peoples' reactions to the
                          \Cycle?

        (Ha! sneaky question. And I'm just
        as sneaky...the answer is c. Ha!)

        I think I'll just slither

     over to the phone and rap with

   the genius about the mechanism that

creates that second reaction...there

are a couple of points...

And that's
how it is done
by the smart ones.

That's how this game is played.

Try it.

87

What your Instructor was giving you...free,
at the beginning of the Rock 'n Roll lecture
was a **Preview** of things-to-come.

The exact same material could have been
given at the end of the class,

and it would have been called a
Summary of things-we-have-had.

Sometimes Instructors won't give
Previews or Summaries, but

they put a "list of topics" or an "outline"
on the board. Like this

Rock 'n Roll Cycle
 1. Functions
 2. Changes
 3. Reactions
 4. Mechanisms
 5. History

I. Rock 'n Roll Cycle
   A. Functions
   B. Changes
   C. Reactions
   D. Mechanisms
II. History

COPY IT....whenever your Instructor puts
a list or an outline on the board...**COPY IT.**

It will give you the Instructor's G-B's
for the Instructor's Exam Questions.

But, you certainly do not need to keep
their 1, 2, 3 and their I-A-B, II-A-B stuff.

It just clutters up the information.

You never had an exam question that
asked for the numbers and letters in
the lecture outline, did you?

The Previews, Summaries, lists, and outlines all train you
to hear the G-B's DURING the class.

And it is an absolute promise to you
that you WILL hear them in class, but only

if, for two weeks,
  you take notes in class,
    do the Fix-ups that night,
      and add in the G-B's that night.

Try it. It's well worth the time.

5

HOW TO GET HELP FROM YOUR TEXTBOOKS

FINDING TEXTBOOK G-B's

When you have to take exams
on your textbook material, you have to

find the textbook G-B's

in order to figure out what
those exam questions will be.

Textbook G-B's, like the lecture/class G-B's,
may be found in several different places

. in SUMMARIES, if they are given,
. in HEADINGS of the section or chapter,
. in INTRODUCTIONS, if they are given.

Let's look, first, for the G-B's in
this **Summary** at the end of a textbook chapter.

Dull...Dull...Dull...

Class systems may be labeled according to the
degree of upward, vertical mobility they permit.
Vertical mobility means movement between classes.
There are several types of class systems.
If a system provides little or no opportunity for
one to improve his/her position, it is called
a caste or caste-like system. If it permits
upward mobility, but only on a selective
basis, it is called an estate system. If
it permits relatively free inter-class
movement, then the system is called open-class.

A textbook summary is like
the "first & last five minutes"
of the Instructor's lecture. You need to
St-Pie it for the
exam question G-B's.

So, why don't you St-Pie
the Summary on your own...
and compare it with
mine on the next page ??

In mine, I circled the textbook G-B's for you.
They are usually in the first two indent levels.

89

```
- class systems
     - (labeled) by degree of upward vertical mobility permitted
          - vertical mobility means movmt. between classes
     - (types)
          - (caste) (caste-like) system
               - provides little or no opport. to improve position
          - (estate) system
               - some upward mobility
                    - only on a selective basis
          - (open-class)
               - relatively free inter-class movmt. permitted
```

This is a proper and okay Summary.
It tells you what things the chapter talked about,

> but it doesn't give you examples or
> explanations for these things...no Pie.

The Pie will be found in the chapter itself and, of
course, it will answer the exam questions on the chapter.

. Name the different TYPES of class systems.
. Does the ESTATE system permit upward mobility?
. How are the class systems LABELED?

HOWEVER.
> The Summaries are likely to be your best chance
> for finding the actual exam question G-B's

because,
sometimes, and sometimes lots of times,
there are difficulties with textbooks & handouts.

. Textbook Headings often cause problems. Sometimes
  they don't <u>exactly</u> relate to the stuff under them.
  Sometimes they really aren't the G-B's because they
  are just stuck in the page to break up a long piece
  of writing.

. And some Introductions don't really give you a preview
  of what's-to-come...they're written to try to catch your
  interest with a lot of "stimulating" questions...which is
  okay, but you usually won't get good
  G-B's from that type of introduction.

they do it to
make you suffer.

They do
NOT.

Do too.

90

Let's look at this list of
section **Headings** from a textbook chapter.

I put the same-meaning words in (circles), [boxes] or underlines.

1) What is meant by Social Class

2) The basis of (Social Class Systems) varies with
   \different societies

3) Class is determined by various factors

4) Two kinds of [Social Mobility]

5) (Class Systems:) three kinds

6) [Social Mobility] in Country Z

7) Stratification affects life chances

8) Myths of a classless society

St-Pie & Clump the Headings and this is what we get ⤸

```
1)  - Social Class
1)      - meaning of
3)      - determined by various factors
2)  - Social Class Systems
2)      - basis varies w/ diff. societies
5)      - kinds (3)
4)  - social mobility
4)      - kinds (2)
6)      - in Country Z
```

```
7) Stratification affects life chances
8) Myths of a classless society
```

Left-over items. I don't
know what to do with them, either.

Don't bother with them.

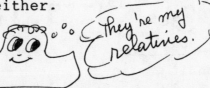

They
sure
are!

It's harder to St-Pie Headings
than to St-Pie Summaries,

> but if you can't get the exam question G-B's
> from your Instructor or from a Summary

⟹ you have to try a St-Pie of the Headings.

Now, about using INTRODUCTIONS
to find the exam question G-B's.
It's a bit of a problem, as I told you.

Sometimes
textbook Introductions are written
to catch your interest & attention,

and they probably do
catch your interest

but they make finding the
exam G-B's very difficult.

For example, here's the kind of
'question introduction' you could
find in a sociology textbook:

> Have you ever wondered why men have developed so
> many different ways of life? Why is it that the
> traveler who wanders from society to society can
> encounter so many fascinating variations in housing,
> diet, art, technology, customs, and the host of other
> items that make up human culture? Since all men
> share a common biological heritage, why have they
> evolved so many different solutions to the problems
> of existence? There are some interesting answers to
> this question.

It's difficult to St-Pie. Messy. You have to turn
all the rhetorical questions into Statements as you go along.
A nuisance.

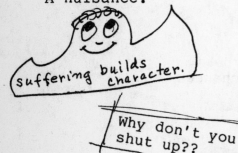

- Men develop
  - different ways of life
- travelers encounter
  - variations in items of culture
    - housing   - diet
    - art   - technology
    - customs   - other items
- men share
  - common biological heritage
    - why diff. solutions to problems?
      - interesting answer to

You could work on it
to find the G-B's, but
with this type of Introduction,
the easiest thing to do is

. read it, and
. take a couple of minutes to see if a quick St-Pie will
                    \turn up the exam question G-B's.
. If not, go look at the chapter Summaries or Headings.

SKIMMING

When you skim something, which you are supposed to
do before you read it,

you get a kind of mental skeleton of what
the stuff is all about...like you know you're
going to get information on the planets and
oceans, but not which ones or what information.

This pays off
in easy grades!

To skim something,
turn the pages and READ

- . the title
- . the first paragraph or two
  - it might have a useful Introduction
- . the first sentence of the paragraphs
  - the author may be writing in a St-Pie
                \pattern giving Statements first
  - just read it...never mind if you don't
                \understand it
- . the headings
- . the captions of the pictures & diagrams
  - just read them...never mind if you don't
                \understand them
- . the summary or concluding paragraph
  - it might have the exam question G-B's

UNDERLINING

..If you underline in your textbooks,
  at least use different colors
                     for your Statements & Pies.

..I hope you do not do
  swoosh underlining???

underlining one line after another,
after another, after another...??
This is not useful.

All it says is, "Oh, my, this feels
important. I'll come back and go over
it before the exam."

..Please do not do this.
  If it feels important, St-Pie it now,
  and tape the St-Pie notes
                     onto the book page, or tape them
                     into your notebook as a Slot-in.

TEXTBOOK ADVICE BOX

1) **Skim** the section or chapter first.

    If you are going to have a lecture on the material in
    the section or chapter, then → BEFORE THE LECTURE,

    skim the material, but do it ALOUD.
    Do it ALOUD 3 times. It will take you
    5 minutes, and wait until you see the
    pay off during the lecture!

                                        Try it.

2) **St-Pie** one of the following: → the SUMMARY, or
                                       the HEADINGS, or
                                       the INTRODUCTION.

        But, remember, none of these things will be
        as reliable as your Instructor

                        → for exam question G-B's

                            ...which is the world's best
                            reason not to cut classes.

3) **Write the G-B's** in the margins of your textbook as you read.

        - If you HAVE TO underline in the textbook, use
          different colors for Statements & Pies.

4) **Match the textbook G-B's** with your lecture/class G-B's,
   and Slot-in to your notes → any NEW information
                                from the textbook.

        Then don't bother with your textbook again.
        But hang onto that notebook!

    <u>The Pay off</u>

        Without any further work you'll have the
        stuff memorized up to a C or C+ grade.

I'm exhausted!

I want to talk
to you. Privately.

??okay.

How to memorize
for the exam is next

95

6

HOW TO MEMORIZE FOR THE EXAM

There are two kinds of things that people have trouble memorizing for exams:

(1) **Large amounts of material**...the big chunks that are too much to keep in your head.

(2) **Hard to memorize** material...the stuff that, even in small amounts, keeps sliding out of your head.

We'll take care of the large amounts problem first.

LARGE AMOUNTS OF MATERIAL

. When you need to memorize large amounts of material in order to get a B or better grade on your exam,

⤷ use the UNITS-OF-FOUR trick.

I'm thinking.

It's easy as Pie.

. Look at your <u>Fixed-Up</u> St-Pie notes, and

wherever you have a string of ⤵

⤷ MORE THAN FOUR items that are lined up VERTICALLY,

like these

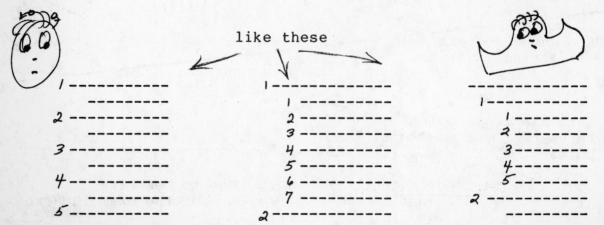

Find a G-B for some of those MORE THAN FOUR items,

and watch what happens!

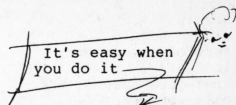

Wanna try it?

It's easy when you do it

like this

St-Pie Notes This stuff (#1-6)	G-B's is talking about	Use the G-B's for Clumping the material
- human hand has		
1 - nails		
2 - thumb		
3 - index finger	a finger	- fingers
4 - middle finger	a finger	- index
5 - ring finger	a finger	- middle
6 - little finger	a finger	- ring
		- little

And the whole thing will fall, kerplunk! right into this

- human hand has
  - nails
  - thumb
  - fingers
    - index
    - middle
    - ring
    - little

where no vertical string of items

has more than four items in it.

Here's another bunch of notes that you would put into Units-of-4 or less...(it makes all your notes easier to learn.)

In these notes, as in most of your notes, you'll want to read the whole St-Pie unit

to pick up the clues for your G-B's

St-Pie Notes This stuff (#1-6) 〵	G-B's is talking about 〵
- types of govnmts	
- Dictatorship	
- one person rule	one person rule
- a form of sovereignty	
- Republic	
- shared government	people share in gov't
- people vote for	
\representatives	
- Absolute Monarchy	
- one person rule	one person rule
- may be hereditary	
- Anarchy	
- each person governs self	no gov't
- no overall govnmnt	
- Oligarchy	
- a group of people rule	group rule
- Democracy	
- shared govnmnt	people share in gov't
- people vote for reps	

Now, use the G-B's for Clumping
the material, ⟶ and see what happens! 〵

```
- types of gov't
   - one person rules
      - Dictatorship
         - a form of sovereignty
      - Absolute Monarchy
         - may be hereditary
   - group of people rule
      - Oligarchy
   - all people share in gov't
      - [ Republic
      - [ Democracy
         - people vote for reps
   - no gov't
      - Anarchy
         - each governs self
```

+ + + + + + + + + + +
+   ADVICE BOX
+
+ Check off each item
+ in your original
+ St-Pie notes as you
+ put it into your
+ Units-of-4 notes.
+ + + + + + + + + + +

Did you manage
that one okay??

Sure. What d'ya'
think we are? Dumb
or somethin'?

Those examples both had the G-B's in their St-Pie units.

Now let's do one where there aren't
any G-B clues in the St-Pie units.

Watch.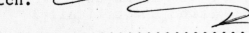

- there are 7 land masses
    - Australia
    - Africa
    - N. America
    - S. America
    - Asia
    - Europe
    - Antarctica

There are no usable
G-B's in these notes.

The Instructor didn't
give us any G-B clues,
just info on each of
the land masses...

and the textbook didn't give
us any clues, either.

So, okay -- we'll
make them up,
because

that's how G-B's for Units-of-Four-or-less
are different from regular G-B's...

you can use <u>anything</u> that comes
into your head for Units-of-4 G-B's

. inside, outside, upside, downside
. left, right, top, bottom, middle
. big, little, medium, medium-little
. size, shape, location, type
. ANYTHING you want. It's your own
                   \private ball game!

So, okay, let's look.
Some of them are
talking about

"tied-together" land masses.

"floating-loose" land masses.

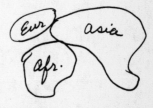

So, okay, I'll use
tied-together & floating loose

as my G-B's,

and Clump the stuff under them.

And now, watch what happens!

```
- 7 land masses
   - tied-together                    Oops!
      - Europe
      - Asia                          Five  items are
      - Africa                        lined up vertically!
      - N. America
      - S. America                    Okay, I'll make up some
   - floating-loose                   G-B's for them...
      - Antarctica
      - Australia                     Aha! "Eastern" & "Western"
                                      land masses will do it!!
                                         Yup!   Watch this
```

St-Pie notes	G-B's	Units-of-4 notes

- 7 land masses
   - tied-together
      - N. America
      - Asia
      - S. America
      - Europe
      - Africa
   - floating-loose
      - Antarctica
      - Australia
	Western
	Eastern
	Western
	Eastern
	Eastern
		- 7 land masses
		   - tied-together
		      - Western
		         - N. America
		         - S. America
		      - Eastern
		         - Asia
		         - Europe
		         - Africa
		   - floating-loose
		      - Antartica
		      - Australia

Kerplunk! right into Units-of-4!

If you want to, you can clump it all into Units-of-4
by using the FIRST LETTERS of the land masses as your G-B's.

Like this

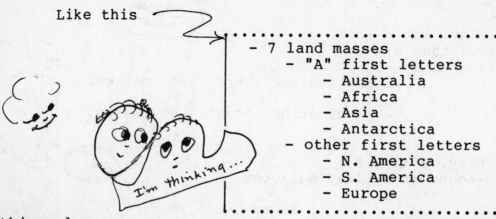

```
- 7 land masses
   - "A" first letters
      - Australia
      - Africa
      - Asia
      - Antarctica
   - other first letters
      - N. America
      - S. America
      - Europe
```

OR use anything else
your mind thinks up.

```
                    ADVICE BOX ON MEMORIZING

IF you are going for a B or better grade,

      you will probably have to memorize large amounts
      of material now and then.  To do this most easily, you

              . St-Pie the G-B's in
                your Units-of-4 organization.

Write it out.  Like this
                                - 7 land masses
                                   - tied-together (5)
                                      - Western  2
                                      - Eastern  3
                                   - floating-loose (2)


The Write-Out will tell you
if anything else needs to be put into Units-of-4.

      It will give you the general, overall exam questions.

AND, as you are writing,
                                your mind is happily pulling
                                all the material together,

                                and effortlessly memorizing
                                between 70%-80% of the material.
```

Units-of-4 is my favorite kind of memorizing,

      because all I have to do is play St-Pie and G-B's
      and Units-of-4, and my mind

            automatically click, click, clicks away,
            happily memorizing great chunks of the material.

There is, of course, a reason
that all this memory happens...

```
+ + + + + + + + INTERESTING INFORMATION + + + + + + + +
+                                                      +
+    If you want to memorize large amounts of          +
+    material                                          +
+              never do the same thing with            +
+                 the same material twice.             +
+                                                      +
+         If you read it the first time, St-Pie        +
+    it the next time.  Then G-B's, then Units-of-4,   +
+    then the Write-Out.                               +
+                                                      +
+                        It works like magic.          +
+                        Try it.  You'll see.          +
+ + + + + + + + + + + + + + + + + + + + + + + + + + + +
```

101

ADVICE BOX ON CONCEPTS

Sometimes you will have
Instructors who want you to "Understand The Concepts"

    or who want you to "Get The Big Picture".
    And, they will tell you, that is what the exam will test.

Do not panic.

- Put your material into Units-of-4.

- St-Pie the G-B's in your
  Units-of-4 organization....Write it out.

        This will give you the Concept/Big Picture exam
        questions your Instructor is talking about.

- Put it ⤴ into sentences. ⤵

The sentences will be "The Concept" or "The Big Picture"
that your Instructor wants you to know.

    <u>Example</u>: (from preceding page)

      "There are seven land masses. Five of these are
      tied together, and two are floating loose. Of the
      five tied together, two are in the Western
      hemisphere and three are in the Eastern hemisphere."

Sneaky, huh?

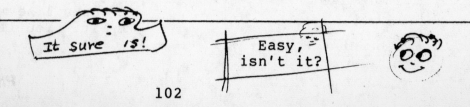

HARD TO MEMORIZE MATERIAL

To memorize this kind of material
   that keeps slipping away from you,

      use these memorizing* tricks

                              ...Making up words
                              ...Sketching
                              ...Charting
                              ...Charting & Sketching

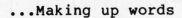...Making up words

      This trick is useful when you have <u>lists</u> of things
      to memorize. For example

(1) if you want to memorize the list of items in the
    human hand:
                    nails, thumb, index finger, middle finger,
                    ring finger, little finger.

   - write down the first
     letter of each item: N T I M R L

   - make up a word, or words, from these letters

                           MR. LINT
                           <u>T</u>I<u>M</u> Loves <u>R</u>ed <u>N</u>ails

         If you want
         to keep the order try   <u>N</u>O<u>T</u> <u>IMMORAL</u>

(2) if you want to memorize the list of different types
    of governments:
                      Dictatorship, Republic, Anarchy,
                      Absolute Monarchy, Oligarchy, Democracy.

   - write down the first
     letter of each type: D R A A O D

   - make up a word, or words, from these letters

                           ROAD AD
                           DAD's OAR
                           A "D" ROAD"

QUESTION BOX: Are you being very smart
                and checking off the letters as you use them?

---

* A memorizing trick is a mnemonic (neh-mon-ik).
  A mnemonic is a device which helps you to memorize.

This trick is useful when you understand the material okay, but the information won't stay in your head. For example

(1) if you have trouble remembering something like this:

"People are affected by psychological, sociological, biological and cultural factors."

(2) if you have trouble with a series of events:

"King William married Queen Grace. They had three children. The first two died and the third one became King of Europe."

or

"The fever bug flies into hot tea and enters the body through the mouth, causing a high fever which penicillin will cure."

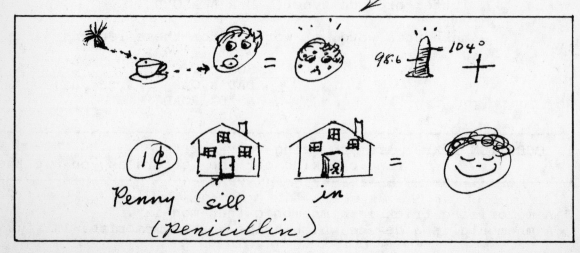

(3) if the subject matter keeps floating away from you,
    sketching as you read will help a lot.

> "Air enters the nose in two streams because the
> nostrils are separated by the septum. From the
> nostrils, air enters the nasal passages which lie
> above the mouth cavity. From the nasal passages
> air passes through the pharynx and enters the
> windpipe, or trachea."

This kind of material
is especially difficult for me.
It is too tightly written, too detailed.
It will not stay in my head. And I can't even
remember it long enough to take the exam, unless I sketch it.
Like this

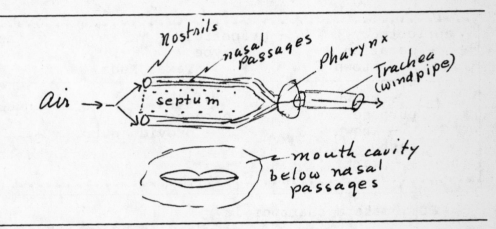

(4) if you have trouble remembering a word like "carbon dioxide"
    make a sketch

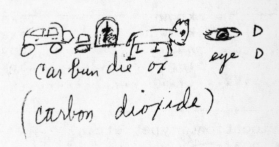

Why don't you try it? Everyone sketches differently.

The important thing about sketching
is that you do it yourself.

> This seems to create a personalized
> imprint of the material into your memory...

> enough to get you through the exam anyway.

105

...Charting

Make a chart when you have to understand or memorize complicated material. The chart makes it clearer, simpler & easier to memorize.

For example, look at this mess of scrambled eggs

"We knew about the location, type and purpose of apricots. The type of grapefruit, however, is Texas Reds. Both apricots and grapefruit have a tart taste, and providing nutrition is the purpose of Texas Reds. However, the apples are from the North; they have a tangy taste."

St-Pie it, and it's still
too scrambled to memorize easily.

```
- apricots             - grapefruit              - apples
   - location            - type                      - location
      - known              - Texas Reds                 - north
   - type                - taste                     - taste
      - known              - tart                       - tangy
   - purpose             - purpose
      - known              - provide nutr.
   - taste
      - tart
```

BUT, make a chart of it
and it becomes easier to memorize.

	APRICOTS	GRAPEFRUIT	APPLES
location	known	Texas *(inferred)*	North
type	known	Texas Reds	(?)
purpose	known	provide nutr.	(?)
taste	tart	tart	tangy

O.K.?

Or make location, type, etc.,
the headings

	LOCATION	TYPE	PURPOSE	TASTE
apricots	known	known	known	tart
grapefruit	Texas	Texas Reds	provide nutr.	tart
apples	North	(?)	(?)	tangy

Mmmm...the missing info...was it given and you missed it? Or was it not given, and are you expected to fill it in from your textbook?

106

```
------------------------------------------------------------
|              ADVICE BOX FOR CHARTING                     |
|                                                          |
|  . Never leave a blank spot in a chart.                  |
|          Put in the information,                         |
|              or fill in the spot with a (?) or (-).      |
|                                                          |
|      (?) means you don't know what goes there.           |
|      (-) means nothing goes there.                       |
|                                                          |
|  . Make charts of everything                             |
|    you can, as often as you                              |
|    can.  Practice.                                       |
|                                                          |
|                        I'm afraid it takes a lot of      |
|                        practice.  But, of course, no one |
|                        is going to shoot you             |
|                        if you don't practice.            |
------------------------------------------------------------
```

Well okay, don't
practice. Just read it
so you know how it's done.

Here's another example.
The material isn't scrambled, but

> if the language keeps
> sliding out of your head,
> even after you've St-Pied it, → try a chart.

"People are affected by various life factors including
psychological factors like personality -- are you calm
or excitable; sociological factors such as wealth -- does
a person have much or little; biological factors such as
sex -- whether one is female or male; and cultural
factors -- whether your environment is urban or rural."

Life Factors Affecting People			
psychological	sociological	biological	cultural
personality - calm - excitable	wealth - much - little	sex - female - male	environment - urban - rural

...If the material still
    keeps sliding out of your head,
    even after you've made a chart, → use the double whammy →

like this

Life Factors Affecting People			
psychological	sociological	biological	cultural
personality - calm	wealth - much	sex - female	environment - urban
- excitable	- little	- male	- rural

ADVICE BOX ON MEMORIZING

It is not smart to keep
going over & over material your mind has already memorized.

   If you want to check out
   what you already know for the exam,

      . make up your questions from your G-B's
      . use scribble notes for your answer
    . check your scribbles with your notes or textbook, and
  . in bright red pen or pencil

write out
what you forgot
or got wrong.

The only things you need to memorize are the bright red spots.

I know that making up charts on all kinds of information
takes time. But it sure helps your grades!

   Try this: read through the material on the next page
              Then look at the same material

                  (plus a lot more)

                          in the chart on the
                                    following page.

You decide if the
material in the chart is clearer and easier to memorize.

Pretend
Pretend

YOU are the Instructor, and
you are explaining to
your class what they
have to do to get
their grades...

"Well," you start, "most students do not seem to know that you get your grades on how you answer the exam questions, NOT on what you know. What you know, or think you know, or know you know but can't explain has no effect at all on your grades."

The happy, eager faces look up in surprised disbelief.

"You should have been taught this in grade school," you continue in a firm voice. "To answer the exam questions well you must, first, know the facts (your St-Pie units). Second, you must know how the facts relate to each other (your G-B's and Units-of-4). Third, you should know The Concepts in the course, The Big Picture. Fourth, you must know how to memorize this material."

You pause. The surprise and disbelief are wilting into a faint glaze of horror. But you carry on.

"You also have to know," you explain, "how to answer exam questions, both objective and essay type questions. If you know the material, objective questions are not difficult. BUT, for essay type questions, you also need to know exactly how much to put into your answer, and how to present the material. For these things you need to know how to write (expository writing). And, of course, you need to know the meaning of the words used in the course (definitions)."

You look at the students. Their faces are blank and placid. They are sitting peacefully, some doodling contentedly in their notebooks, some gazing thoughtfully at a spot above your head. They are not listening. They have calmly, during that last paragraph, wiped out everything you have said, the course itself, and you as their Instructor.

"Naturally," you explain quickly, "you don't have to do ALL of it just to pass the course."

Too late. You should have put it onto the board as a chart, and not scared them to death.

Here is what you just told your class

(plus a lot more)

put into a chart.

Your grade depends on how you answer the exam questions, NOT on what you know.						
This is what you do	**(which we call)**	to help you get these grades				
		A	B	C	D	E
Know the facts	St-Pie units	x	x	x	x	-
Know how the facts relate to each other	G-B's	x	x	x	-	-
Memorize the material	Units-of-4	x	x	-	-	-
	Chart, Sketch	x	x	-	-	-
Know the Concepts or The Big Pix	St-Pie the G-B's in your Units-of-4 organization	x	-	-	-	-
Know how to answer exam Q's – objective	Memorize the material	(see above)				
– essay	Expository writing	x	x	x	-	-
Know the exact meanings of the words	Definitions	x	(?)	-	-	-
No. of tricks to be learned to get each grade		7	5	3	1	0

I'm going to take a nap.

110

7

HOW TO ANSWER THE EXAM QUESTIONS
&
- HOW TO WRITE -

There are two kinds of exam questions:

. **Objective questions**

> in which you select an answer
> out of the choices offered to you.

. **Essay questions**

> in which you make up an answer
> out of what is in your head.

There are several
books in the bookstores
on how to answer objective questions of all types.

    They give you very good advice, and
        strategies for dealing with these questions,
            along with plenty of examples
                and dozens of exercises,
                        so there's no point
                            in my doing it, too.

The author is lazy.

I am not!

You are, too.

They can get it in a bookstore.

They won't go.

Yes, they will.

No, they won't.

You can find these
books on objective questions
in a bookstore or in a library.

> Pick one you like, then
> work through it slowly,
> alone or with some friends.

>> It's sort of fun, and it
>> can pay off in better grades.

We'll do the essay type question now.

You already know, probably,
that different students answer
an essay question differently.

There is the free flowing, I-am-creative student who answers it like this	There is the sudden-brilliant-thought student who answers it like this
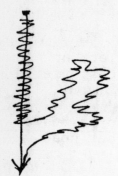	
and gets a D grade.	and gets a C grade.

Both kinds of students
seem to feel their
creativity is strangled
if they are asked to
write a simple, direct,
organized answer, like this

which gets an A or B grade.

When you want a high grade
on an essay question, you should use

the organization of

expository writing.

The purpose of this kind of writing
is to convey information in a

clear, precise

and _familiar_ form of organization.

This is the form of organization that your Instructors
know about and expect to see in your essay question answers.

It is also the form of organization that is required
for _everything_ you are asked to do in school.

..When you are asked

(to)   (to)

explain   talk
discuss   give a speech
compare   answer a question
contrast   use communication skills

(to write)

a theme   a summary
a paper   a memo (memorandum)
a precis   the answer to a question

you are being asked to present
your material in the organization form
that is used in the expository writing of a theme.

You are not using this form
if your themes and essay questions   get criticisms like these

"Conclusion is weak."

"Organization needs more work."

"Argument is weak."   "Introduction is weak."

"Paragraph development is weak."

My themes used to get criticisms like that.
It sounded as if I did poor work on purpose.

It made me mad.

It took me a long time to figure out
what to do so that every single thing in my themes

    ✓ Introduction, Thesis
    ✓ Sentence, Conclusion,
    ✓ paragraph development   ✓✓ was absolutely
    ✓ organization, body, etc.   right.

                      (After that I got higher grades
                        even when I knew less material!!)

This is what I figured out:

        A theme is nothing but a bunch of
        Statements & Pies put together in different ways

             to make up the three (3) different sections
             of a theme...Introduction, Body & Conclusion.

THE INTRODUCTION

  .. is made up of two things

    - a Thesis Sentence...which is a (Statement) you make up
                               in a particular way.

    - a Skeleton Summary...which is a series of (Statements)
                      you make up in a particular way.

THE BODY

  .. is made up of one thing

    - a series of (Statement-Pie Units)...which relate to the
                                Thesis Sentence in
                               a particular way.

THE CONCLUSION

  .. is made up of two OR three things

       ┌ Thesis Sentence
    - a │   &
       └ Skeleton Summary ...which are the same (Statements)
                       that are in the Introduction;
                       they can be written in any
                       order you want.

       ┌ discussion
    - a │   or
       └ evaluation ...which is used ONLY if asked for by
                       your Instructor.

First we will look at the Body of the theme,
because that is where everything else comes from.

The BODY of a theme is just a series of St-Pie units.

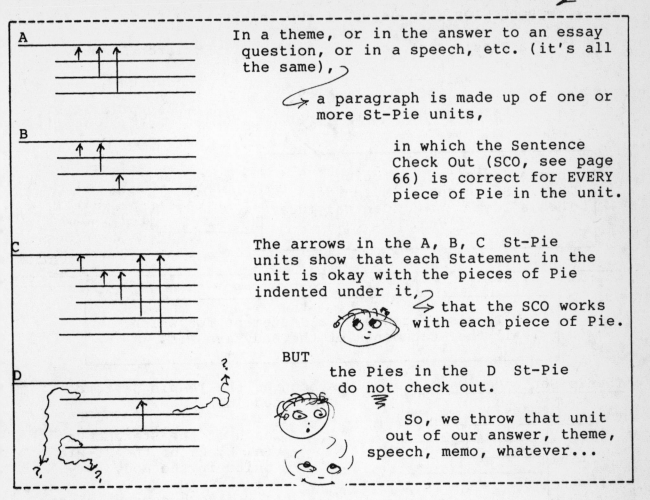

In a theme, or in the answer to an essay question, or in a speech, etc. (it's all the same),

a paragraph is made up of one or more St-Pie units,

in which the Sentence Check Out (SCO, see page 66) is correct for EVERY piece of Pie in the unit.

The arrows in the A, B, C St-Pie units show that each Statement in the unit is okay with the pieces of Pie indented under it, that the SCO works with each piece of Pie.

BUT

the Pies in the D St-Pie do not check out.

So, we throw that unit out of our answer, theme, speech, memo, whatever...

ADVICE BOX ON ORGANIZING

Any time you have a piece of Pie where the SCO shows it is NOT Pie for the Statement,

take a deep breath, and

✓ throw out that piece of Pie, or

✓ change the Pie to fit the St, or

✓ change the St to fit the Pie, or

are you allowed to do that?

Nobody will know.

✓ keep it for another theme, memo, speech, etc.

If you leave it in, even though the SCO warned you it didn't fit, you will be criticized for "poor organization"

"not sticking to the subject"

"weak argument"

The second thing to look at is the Introduction.

The INTRODUCTION is made up of two things:

..a Thesis Sentence   and   ..a Skeleton Summary

which   which

has many names   we'll look at next.

Thesis Sentence	Topic
Thesis Statement	Main Idea
Thesis Idea	Central Idea
etc.	

why don't they make up their minds?

A Thesis Sentence is a Statement for which
all the Statements of the Body are Pie.

Thesis Sentence (Th.S.)

A

St-Pie unit = OK

B

St-Pie unit = OK

C

D *We threw this one out — remember?*

As soon as the Thesis Sentence
is added in,

each of the Statements
(A, B, C) of the St-Pie
units in the Body

also becomes a piece
of Pie for the Th.S.
(Thesis Sentence).

The arrows here show that A & B
in the Body are okay as Pies for
the Th.S.,

that the SCO works with
both of them.

BUT

look at the C St-Pie unit.
It is okay by itself as a St-Pie
unit. The SCO works on it.

It is NOT okay as a piece of Pie
for the Th.S. The SCO does not
work on it, and if C is not
Pie for the Th.S...

THROW IT OUT!

Try covering up the Thesis Sentence line on the preceding page.

If you look at St-Pie units A & B
WITHOUT the Thesis Sentence,

you see that they are isolated, separate pieces
of information. Pretend that

the Statement for A says: "Applesauce is good" &
the Statement for B says: "Palm trees in the tropics".

A Thesis Sentence is the thing that
ties together isolated St-Pie units.

Th.S.: <u>Applesauce is good to eat while sitting</u>
        <u>under the palm trees in the tropics.</u>

Or, suppose you have
three St-Pie units, and the
                            3rd Statement says: "Teacher".

You could tie them all together
with a Th.S., like this

Th.S.: <u>The teacher ate the good applesauce while</u>
        <u>discussing palm trees in the tropics.</u>

Neat, huh?

ADVICE BOX ON FINGER-POINTING

Do you know about Finger-Pointing????

Whenever you are reading **material that has a reference to
something else**, like a diagram,
                                      use your fingers:

put one finger on the item in the <u>material</u>,
    and one finger on the item in the <u>reference</u>.

<u>Example:</u>
            When I said, in the preceding page, "...look at
            C St-Pie unit, you would put

            one finger on the letter C in the <u>material</u>
            & one finger on the letter C in the <u>reference</u>.

                                    (the diagram)

It takes two hands. It works GREAT for all kinds of directions.

Now, let's do the second thing that goes into the Introduction.

The INTRODUCTION is made up of two things:

~~a Thesis Sentence~~   &   a Skeleton Summary

A Skeleton Summary (SS) is a <u>shortened</u>
list of the Statements of the Body (A, B, C, etc.),

IN THE ORDER OF THEIR APPEARANCE IN THE BODY.

St-Pie Notes   Written Out As A Theme

THESIS SENTENCE (TH.S.)   INTRODUCTION   (TH.S. & SS)

<u>The USA is a great country.</u>   <u>The USA is a great country.</u>

SKELETON SUMMARY (SS)

politics   This fact is shown by its
social system   politics, its social system,
education   and the education it offers.

BODY   BODY (St-Pie units in order of SS)

<u>politics is not bad</u>   Politics in the USA is
_____   very good. There are free
_____   elections, and free speech
_____   about the candidates...pie...
                                       pie...pie...

<u>social system = democratic</u>   The social system is
_____   democratic. Even if you are
_____   born poor, like Lincoln, you
_____   can become...pie...pie...pie...

<u>education = quite good</u>   Education is quite good
_____   though it is not perfect.
_____   Children have a right to a
_____   free education up through high
                                       school...pie...pie...pie...

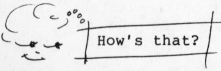

How's that?

Not too bad.

I like it.

The next thing is the Conclusion

118

The CONCLUSION is made up of two OR three things:

the **Thesis Sentence**   &   an **Evaluation**
  & **Skeleton Summary**

The Thesis Sentence (Th.S.) and Skeleton Summary (SS) are the same ones as in the Introduction, BUT they can be written ➥ IN ANY ORDER YOU WANT.	An evaluation or a point of view or a discussion, ➥ IF IT IS ASKED FOR IN THE ASSIGNMENT.

St-Pie Notes ↘   Written As A Theme ↘

CONCLUSION   CONCLUSION

Skeleton Summary (SS)
    \in any order

- **social system**   The **social system**, the
- **education**   **education** and the **politics**
- **politics**   in the USA all indicate that

Thesis Sentence (Th.S.)   <u>the USA is a great country.</u>

Evaluation (if asked for)   I think the political freedom and
                                       the **educational** opportunities
                                       are particularly great.

Well?   It's easier than our old way.   I like it!

ADVICE BOX ON INTRODUCTIONS

<u>SITUATION</u>	<u>SOLUTION</u>
Some Instructors want the Introduction to be one sentence. ⟋	Combine the Th. S. and the SS into one sentence.
Some want the Introduction to be more than one sentence. ⟋	Put the Th.S. and the SS into separate sentences.
Some want <u>only</u> the Th.S. in the Introduction. ⟋	Make the Th.S. the first paragraph, and the SS the second paragraph.

The only way to know what to do is to listen for the
    clues from each Instructor. If you don't get any
clues -- look at the comments on everyone's papers when
    the first theme or essay-question exam is handed back.

ADVICE BOX ON WRITING PARAGRAPHS

...When you are writing your paragraphs, follow this chart

If your theme size is	Do this with the St-Pie units in the Body
very short	combine all the units into one paragraph
average	make each unit a separate paragraph
very long	make each unit several paragraphs, using each Pie as one paragraph

ADVICE BOX ON ANSWERING ESSAY QUESTIONS

...When you are answering a
  question, or explaining something, or
  writing a theme, or giving a speech, etc.

It's okay.

            use either a

  St-Pie pattern   or   Pie-St pattern

"The USA is a good country.   "If we look at its politics,
This fact is shown in its   its social system and its
politics, its social system   education, we can see that
and the education it offers."   the USA is a good country."

A fancy name for   A fancy name for
the St-Pie pattern   the Pie-St pattern
of thinking is   of thinking is
"Deductive reasoning."   "Inductive reasoning."

            Unless you are <u>very</u> skilled
              at this writing business
        don't fool around with the Pie-St-Pie pattern.

Sometimes people want to use the Pie-St-Pie pattern because they
want to "vary the sentence structure" or they want to write
  with "style". If you feel you must use the Pie-St-Pie,

    keep your Introduction, Conclusion & Body separated by
                  paragraphs, and
    keep the Statements of the Body in the order you gave
                in your Skeleton Summary.

            Now, try writing an essay answer.

Well. Okay. I'll do it myself.

Suppose I have to answer the question:
"Why are Personal Computers (PCs) an important industry?"

Or I have to write a theme, or give a talk,
or whatever, on: "The importance of the PC industry."

FIRST I make my St-Pie notes. THEN I write it out.

PCs = important industry
- make jobs for people
  - manufacturers hire people
    - to make hardware
                &
              software
  - retail stores hire people
    - to sell PCs
    - give advice on software
  - service people
    - repair hardware
    - teach use of software
- make people happy
  - like to use computers for
    - writing
    - studying
    - fun & games

→ S.S.
→ Th.S.

Personal Computers (PCs) are an important industry because they make jobs for people & make people happy.

They make jobs for the people the manufacurers hire to make the hardware and the software. Retail stores also hire people to sell the PCs and advise customers on the software. Service people who repair computers or teach others to use the software get jobs. Especially, the PCs make people happy. People like using them for writing, studying and for fun & games.

Making jobs for people & making people happy seem to be two reasons why PCs are an important industry.

121

The theme on the last page is <u>perfectly organized</u>.

It may not be interesting;
it may sound repetitious;
and the ideas in it may be dumb.....but it is absolutely,
                                    perfectly A+ organized.

When you write short answers or themes
they will sound repetitious, but don't worry about it.

The repetition will disappear when
   your themes, answers, etc. get longer.

And remember, you aren't
   trying to be "a writer".
   You are just trying to

      put down what you know
         in the organization pattern

      your Instructor wants
                  so you can get the
                              grade you want.

ADVICE BOX ON ANSWERING ESSAY QUESTIONS

. You need to actually see

      how many WORDS you write in 10 minutes, and
      how much SPACE your writing covers in 10 minutes,

         when you are <u>writing from St-Pie notes.</u>

. . . .

   This will give you a <u>visual picture</u> of the
   amount of space you can fill in 10 minutes.

      Example: 1/4 of a page = 10 minutes

   It will also give you a visual picture of
   the amount of space that <u>a particular number</u>
   <u>of your written words</u> takes up.

      Example: 1/4 of a page = 50 words

When you know this   you can then figure out that

      . if the question asks you to write about 100 words,
            you will need to fill up about 1/2 the page, and

         . if the question says to spend 30 minutes on it,
            you will need to fill up 3/4 of a page.

The essay question will give you either

     the number of words that is wanted   (e.g., 50-75 words)
or   the amount of time you should spend (e.g., 10-15 minutes).

If you don't know how much space 50-75 words will cover, and
you don't know how much space you can fill in 10-15 minutes

...how will you know when and where to stop??

WHAT GOES INTO YOUR ESSAY QUESTION ANSWER?

     ...What kind of information: Statements or Pies or both?
     ...How much of each kind?

(I don't believe it.)

          Easy as Pie...!
          Just follow this chart

CHART FOR ANSWERING ESSAY QUESTIONS			
(20-30 words) 2-5 minutes	(50-75 words) 10-15 minutes	(100-150 words) 20-30 minutes	(300-500 words) 45-60 minutes

Introduction
- Th.S.
 	
Body
- St #1
 	
- St #2
 	
- St #3
 	
Conclusion
 	
(none)
	Introduction
	- Th.S.
	
	Body
	- St #1
	   - Pie
	
	- St #2
	   - Pie
	
	- St #3
	   - Pie
	
	Conclusion
	
	(none)
		Introduction
		- Th.S.
		- SS
		Body
		- St #1
		   - Pie
		   - Pie
		- St #2
		   - Pie
		   - Pie
		- St #3
		   - Pie
		   - Pie
		Conclusion
		- Th.S.
		- SS
		(- Discussion
		   if asked
		   for)
			Introduction
			- Th.S.
			- SS
			Body
			- St #1
			   - Pie
			   - Pie
			   - Pie
			- St #2
			   - Pie
			   - Pie
			   - Pie
			- St #3
			   - Pie
			   - Pie
			   - Pie
			Conclusion
			- Th.S.
			- SS
			(- Discussion
			   if asked
			   for)

..You can use 50% of the time allowed for the question
   to recall the information & organize your answer.

          That's where the work is.

          Writing the answer is easy.

Most people use the "bruised knee" approach. They put their pencil on the paper, get on their knees and pray.

It is not a good system.

The four-step system is much better

✓ analyze the question
✓ recall the information
✓ organize the information
✓ write the answer

There are two types of people who don't use this system... geniuses and people who never heard about it.

To analyze the question:

..St-Pie the question as best you can. Use Scribble Notes.

..Draw this balloon symbol beside any piece of the St-Pie notes that you have to answer.

..When you have put in all the balloons, go back and put a number in each one.

Example:

Instructor's Question:

The two books, TODAY'S WORLD and OUR WORLD TODAY, are trying to tell us something. What is the message of each; what do they have in common; how do they differ? State your reason for agreeing or disagreeing with the book OUR WORLD TODAY.

St-Pie notes	Scribble notes
2 books trying tell us something	2 bks try tell smthng
- message	- msge
- bk A	- bk A ①
- bk B	- B ②
- things in common	- thngs commn
-	- .... ③
- differences	- diffs
-	- .... ④
- reason for [agree with or disagree w/] bk B	- rsn agree/dis B
	- .... ⑤

To recall the information:

..Make scribble notes on a scrap of paper,
or in the margins of the question sheet they gave you.

..Pieces of information will float up into your
mind as you scribble. Continue making scribble
notes until nothing more floats up.

..Attach balloon numbers to your recall scribbles.

Example:

DO NOT ATTEMPT TO ORGANIZE MATERIAL AS LONG
AS INFORMATION IS FLOATING UP INTO YOUR MIND.

If you try to organize it at this stage
you will cut off the flow of recall.

To organize the information:

..St-Pie your recall scribbles   USE SCRIBBLE NOTES PLEASE.

Write the balloon numbers, and St-Pie under them.
OR Write the balloon words, and St-Pie under them.

Example:

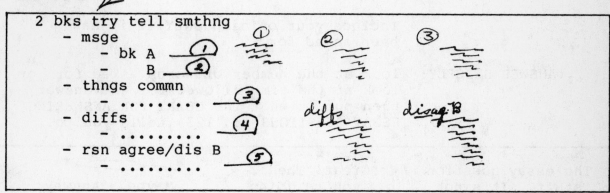

NOW   write the answer to the question.

This system requires practice before the exam. You can
practice when you are checking out what you have already
memorized: (1) Ask yourself a G-B question on your
material, and (2) use these four steps to answer it.

ADVICE BOX ON ANSWERING ESSAY QUESTIONS

Include the question in your answer whenever you can.

Do this in the first sentence of your answer.
It keeps you on track, and pleases the Instructor.

<u>Example</u>: (using p. 125 "organize the information")

- The message of (book A) TODAY'S WORLD is..........
- The message of (book B) OUR WORLD TODAY is........
- The things that the two books have in common are..
- The two books differ on the following topics......
- My reason for agreeing with OUR WORLD TODAY is....

The following words usually have the following meanings:

..COMPARE: give the similarities AND differences.

..DESCRIBE: give the St-Pie information about it.

..DISCUSS: give the St-Pie information AND your opinion.

..WRITE A SUMMARY: give the Thesis Sentence AND the
Statements of the Body.

Include your opinion ONLY if it has
been asked for.

..ANSWER BRIEFLY: look at the number of words asked for, or
look at the time allowed for the answer,
then put in what the CHART FOR ANSWERING
ESSAY QUESTIONS (p. 123) tells you to.

The essay question stuff. It's not bad.

Great! Then you're going to use it?

Maybe. Anyway, I think we're ready to go now.

I want to know about Outlines.

what for?!

I have to write them with themes. In school.

Okay.

Here's how to make OUTLINES.

TO MAKE A TOPIC OUTLINE...two steps:

(1) make your St-Pie notes,

(2) erase the dashes & put in outline numbers and letters.

```
┌─────────────────────┐          ┌─────────────────────┐
│ (1) ST-PIE NOTES    │          │ (2) TOPIC OUTLINE   │
└─────────────────────┴──────────┴─────────────────────┘
```

(1) ST-PIE NOTES	(2) TOPIC OUTLINE
PCs = important industry	I. PCs = important industry
- make jobs for people	A. make jobs for people
- manufacturers hire people	1. mnf'ers hire people
- to make hardware	a. to make hardware
&	&
software	software
- retail stores hire people	2. retailers hire people
- to sell PCs	a. to sell PCs
- give advice on software	b. to advise on sftw.
- make people happy	B. make people happy
- like to use computers for	1. like comptrs for
- writing	a. writing
- studying	b. studying
- fun & games	c. fun & games

TO MAKE A SENTENCE OUTLINE...add step three:

. write the Topic Outline in full sentences.

```
                              ┌─────────────────────────┐
                              │ (3) SENTENCE OUTLINE    │
                              └─────────────────────────┘
```

I. Personal Computers (PCs) are an important industry.
  A. They make jobs for people.
    1. Manufacturers hire people for Personal Computer work.
      a. The people make hardware and software for the PCs.
    2. Retail stores hire people for Personal Computer work.
      a. The people sell PCs and give advice on software.
  B. They make people happy.
    1. People like to use the computers.
      a. They like to write with computers.
      b. They like to study with computers.
      c. They like computers for fun and games.

That's all there is to it.

Now let's do some definitions.

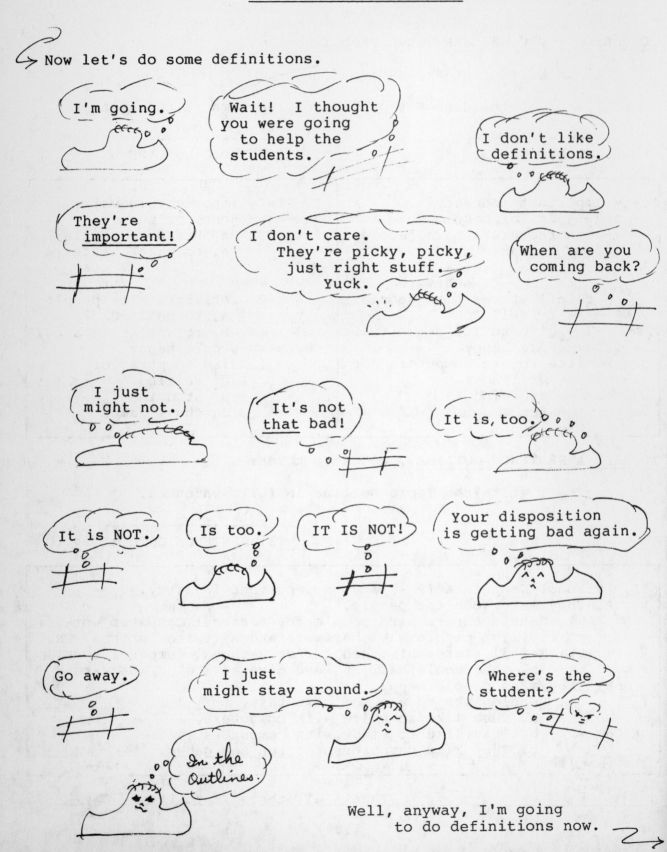

Well, anyway, I'm going
to do definitions now.

Everytime your Instructors
or textbooks use a new word,   they define it.

        They tell you what the new word means

                because they don't dare say, "Twerps
                are common in every group", and

                    then not tell you what a Twerp is.

A definition
has two purposes.....(1) is to distinguish an item from
                        all other items in the Universe,

                    .....(2) is to establish between
                                the Instructor & the class, or
                                the writer & the reader, or
                                the speaker & the listener
                        exactly what will be meant when a
                        particular word is used between them.

        The purpose of (1) is to isolate.
        The purpose of (2) is to communicate.

A definition
is a statement of the meaning of a particular word.

        This statement of what a word means can,
        and usually does, vary from Instructor to Instructor

                    and textbook to textbook. That's just
                    the way the game is played.

A definition has four parts

(1)	(2)	(3)	(4)
You NAME the item you are going to define.	You say, "IS A" or "IS THE"	You give its CATEGORY or CLASSIFICATION	You give the FACTOR that makes this item DIFFERENT from all others in its Category or Classific.
One	is a	single digit number	which immediately follows zero.
Two	is a	single digit number	which immediately follows one.

Okay??  Here are some definitions from
Biology,
Computers, &
Space

name	"is a"	category	difference factor
A cell	is a	mass of protoplasm	which is the smallest biological unit able to function independently.
A tissue	is a	group of cells	all serving the same biological function.
A database	is a	collection of data	stored in a computer.
Programming	is the	process	of writing instructions for a computer.
Intergalactic space	is the	region	between the galaxies.

A definition
can, and usually will,

> vary from Instructor to Instructor,
> and from textbook to textbook.

Example: You are taking two semesters of Biology. You
have different Instructors for each semester.
You better watch it, or you'll be in trouble.

Instructor #1 →

A cell	is the	smallest biological unit	that can function independently.

Instructor #2 →

A cell	is a	mass of protoplasm	which is the smallest biological unit that can function independently.

...and you know what happens to your grade
when you say a cell is the smallest biological
unit,
and your Instructor wanted you to
say it was a mass of protoplasm.

And the same thing will happen
if you mix up definitions
from different courses.

Example

Power	is the	position	of ascendency over others.
Power	is the	ability	to produce an effect.

 Course #1 →
Course #2 →

...if your Instructor says power is an
ability and you say it's a position,

you will lose the ability to
catch the grade you want to
have.

That's just the way the game is played...

So, listen for
    your <u>Instructor's</u> definitions,
        just as you listened for your Instructor's G-B's.

Sometimes your Instructor
will make the definition fancy, like this

Power	is the	position	of ascendency over others.
Power	is that	position	in which one has ascendency over others.
Power	is that	ability	because of which one is able to produce an effect.
Power	is the	ability	to produce an effect.

Regular →
Fancy →
Very Fancy →
Regular →

Sometimes the
Instructors and textbooks
don't know how to write a definition.

They use "<u>is when</u>" definitions:

> Power is when one has ascendency over others.
> Power is when you are able to produce an effect.

They use "<u>is called</u>" definitions:

> Ascendency over others is called Power.
> Producing an effect is called Power.

They use "<u>colon (:)</u>" definitions:

> Power: to have ascendency over others.
> Power: producing an effect.

> They do everything except tell you
> what Power is. With those definitions
> Power could be a look, an act, a
> feeling, a desire...anything.

There is absolutely nothing
you can do about an Instructor's incorrect definitions.

✓ Do NOT tell your Instructor

> that the definition is incomplete,
> that the category/classification is missing.

✓ Get the corrrect definition for yourself, if you can.

> It will speed up your reading comprehension
> and it will make your exam taking easier.

✓ BUT, use the Instructor's definition on the exam.

ADVICE BOX FOR REGULAR DEFINITIONS

100% OF THE TIME, use IS A or IS THE after the item. *← For yourself.*
This forces you to name the category.

100% OF THE TIME, use YOUR INSTRUCTOR's definitions. *← For the exam.*
Even if you know they aren't exactly correct.

Did you know that about Instructors?

No. I thought everything was my fault.

But it isn't.

> The Advice Box on the next page is necessary for Science
> and Math students, but anyone who wants to can read it.

132

ADVICE BOX FOR SCIENCE & MATH STUDENTS

In science and math courses,
words are defined differently than in other courses.

Other courses, like history, psychology, English, etc.,
almost always use **descriptive definitions**,

↪ like those given up to here.

But science & math courses
almost always use **operational definitions**, which can be stated

↪ <u>in words</u> or
<u>as an equation</u>.

Example: POWER

 Descriptive definition: Power is the ability to produce
        an effect.

 Operational definition:
  <u>in words</u>...   Power is the time rate of doing work.

  <u>as an equation</u>... $P = W/t$

Example: AREA OF A RECTANGLE

 Descriptive definition: The area of a rectangle is the
        amount of surface included
        within the rectangle.

 Operational definition:
  <u>in words</u>...   The area of a rectangle is the
        length multiplied by the width.

  <u>as an equation</u>... $A = L \times W$

Example: PERIMETER OF A RECTANGLE

 Descriptive definition: The perimeter of a rectangle is the
        outer border of the rectangle.

 Operational definition:
  <u>in words</u>...   The perimeter of a rectangle is the
        sum of the lengths of the four sides.

  <u>as an equation</u>... $p = 2L + 2W$

An operational definition of an item is a
definition which tells you the **operation**
that **must** be performed in order to find
that item.

133

9

WRITING PROBLEMS ... and SOLUTIONS

Transition Sentences: problem & solution.

A Transition Sentence is a sentence which tells the reader that you are going to move from one idea to another.

When you have a Transition Sentence Problem, your Instructor writes comments like these ⟍⟶ on your papers.

(Transitions poor)   (Organization weak)

(Needs more work)

When you want to get rid of the problem, you use ⟍⟶ Linking Words.

.. The Skeleton Summary words of the Introduction (p. 118) ⟶ are the Linking Words.

.. Each of these SS Linking Words ⟶ must also appear UNCHANGED in the Body & Conclusion.

Example: ↴

If you use **social class** in the SS of the Introduction, you also use **social class** in the Body, and **social class** in the SS of the Conclusion.

Some people may tell you that using <u>different</u> words will give your writing "more variety". They think you should use ⟶ **fringe benefits** in the SS of the Intro,
extra benefits in the Body, and
hidden salary   in the SS of the Concl.

...I don't advise it. But you can try it if you want.

(Well, that's not hard.)   (Could I get A's with Linking Words?)   (You could get B's easy as Pie. There's more.)

(I just might want an A sometime...)

... **EACH** Linking Word appears, unchanged, in the Body
　　　in the <u>1st sentence</u> of the
　　　　　<u>paragraph</u> that starts talking about it.

　　the 1st Linking Word in the <u>1st sentence</u> of the
　　2nd Linking Word in the <u>1st sentence</u> of the
　　3rd Linking Word in the <u>1st sentence</u> of the *— etc.*

... **ALL** the Linking Words appear, unchanged, in the Conclusion.

　　They are the Skeleton Summary of the Conclusion.
　　They appear anywhere, in any order, in the Conclusion.

... In the <u>1st sentence</u> of the Conclusion we put in Conclusion
　Signal <u>Words</u>, like these

And that's all you have to do.

Therefore,.......
To summarize,..........
From this brief look we can see.....
Because of these things...........

Then add in the S.S.

A theme **WITHOUT** Linking Words in the Body

　　Our teacher, Mr. Skwitch, is a colorful character. He is
<u>**funny**</u>, <u>**very persistent**</u>, and has a <u>**terrible temper**</u>.
　　His humor shows when he tells jokes to explain the math
problems. He also sticks to his guns. He never lets up on
giving us homework because he says if we don't practice using
our brains, smart politicians will make mince meat out of us.
It makes him angry when students talk during class, and he
yells, "You have no right to keep other people from getting
an education!"
　　Because of these things -- his irritability, his humor
and his stubbornness -- he is considered a colorful character.

---

and **WITH** Linking Words in the Body.

　　Our teacher, Mr. Skwitch, is a colorful character. He is
<u>**funny**</u>, <u>**very persistent**</u>, and has a <u>**terrible temper**</u>.
　　He seems <u>**funny**</u> to us because he always tells jokes to
explain the math problems. He is also <u>**very persistent**</u>. He
never lets up on giving us homework because he says if we
don't practice using our brains, smart politicians will make
mince meat out of us. His <u>**terrible temper**</u> bursts out when
students talk during class, and he yells, "You have no right
to keep other people from getting an education!"
　　Because of these things -- his <u>**terrible temper**</u>, being
<u>**funny**</u> and being <u>**very persistent**</u> -- he is considered a
colorful character.

It's easier!

The Thesis Sentence: problem & solution.

 The usual way for people to blow it
when they answer essay questions or write themes

is to write a Thesis Sentence
where one part of it has no Pie in the Body.

... This is guaranteed to
lower your grades every time.

Example: (The Thesis Sentence will be underlined.)

Introduction

<u>We in the USA are better off than people in many other</u>
<u>countries.</u> We have open democratic elections, freedom
of religion, and free education through high school.

Body

...the Body develops the three items in the Skeleton
Summary, using good Pie and Transition Sentences with
Linking Words.

Problem

No Pie in the Body for <u>many other countries.</u>

Solution

. Throw out <u>many other countries</u> from the Thesis Sentence.
. Cut back the Thesis Sentence so it covers only the
Skeleton summary items.

<u>The USA is a great country in several ways.</u>

A good way to check out
your Thesis Sentence

is to actually scribble down the Statements (Sts)
that you made in the Thesis Sentence (Th.S.),

for which you will need Pie.

Example:

Th.S. → <u>Our teacher, Mr. Skwitch, is a colorful character.</u>

Sts →   1. Teacher, Mr. Skwitch, is a colorful character.

      Your Instructor will expect Pie for
      this one statement.

. . . .

Th.S. → <u>Our teacher, Mr. Skwitch, is the most colorful
character in our school.</u>

Sts →   1. Our teacher is a colorful character.
      2. Other teachers are not as colorful.
      3. Staff people are not as colorful.

(yuck.)

      Your Instructor will expect Pie for
      these THREE statements!

So why not throw out <u>the most</u> from
your Thesis Sentence, and make it easy on yourself
to write your theme or answer your essay question ??

↪ <u>Our teacher, Mr. Skwith, is a colorful character.</u>

The trick is to cut back your Thesis Sentence
so you don't have to do so much work...

Example:

If you have this Thesis Sentence

<u>There are more health-related career opportunities today
than ever before.</u>

      You have to find Pie for

      1. Health-related career opportunities today.
      2. Health-related career opportunities before.

But, if you cut back your Thesis Sentence to

<u>There are many health-related career opportunities today.</u>

      You only have to find Pie for

      1. Health-related career opportunities today.

Sometimes you will write a perfectly good
Thesis Sentence, and then mess it up

> by putting a fancy addition onto
> one of your Skeleton Summary items,

>> for which there is no Pie
>> in the Body.

Example:

In the USA there are some good and some bad things. We
have a beautiful land; not everyone has a good standard
of living; and our government is good compared to others.

.. The Thesis Sentence is okay.

.. But, if you leave in "compared to others"

you'll make extra work for yourself...

exactly the same work as if
you had put "compared to others"
in the Thesis Sentence.

.. You will not only have to Pie our gov't is good,

but you will ALSO have to

1. Give Pie for the gov't of other countries.
2. Compare their gov'ts with ours.
3. Discuss why ours is better. Yuck!

If 1,2,3 are not done...your Instructor will
make comments on your papers

"Paragraph development is weak."

"You fail to support your argument." "Needs more work."

Choose one:

. You can cut back your Thesis Sentence and Skeleton
  Summary,

do a small amount of work on
your modest Thesis Sentence,
and get a B.

. You can look up all the extra information you must
  have,

write & write and work & work
on your fancy Thesis Sentence,
and get a B.

The Conclusion: problem & solution.

The Conclusion Problem

is exactly the same as the
Thesis Sentence Problem: ┐

↳ One part of it has
no Pie in the Body.

It just happens at the other end
of your essay answer or theme.

Example: ↙

Introduction

The USA is a country with many freedoms. It has freedom
of religion, freedom of elections, and it offers free
education through the high-school years.

Body

...the Body develops the three Skeleton Summary items,
using good Pie & Transition Sentences with Linking Words.

CONCLUSION

In conclusion, the USA is <u>one of the best countries in
the world to live in</u> because of its free education, free
elections and freedom of religion.

Problem

↳ No Pie in the Body for "one of the...to live in".

Solution: You have a choice between (1) or (2).

(1) In the Body you can

- describe the education, elections and religion
\of several other countries,   AND

- compare them with the USA education, etc.

(2) In the Conclusion you can

- throw out "one of the...to live in",   AND
- cut back the Conclusion to cover only the items
↙ in the Introduction.

Easy!

<u>The USA is a country with many freedoms: free education, etc.</u>

Okay?   Here's one more Conclusion Problem example.

Introduction

The USA is a country where people express many different beliefs about government, education and the environment.

Body

...the Body develops the three Skeleton Summary items, using good Pie & Transition Sentences with Linking Words.

CONCLUSION

From this brief look at the USA, it seems that this is a <u>strong and powerful</u> country where people express many different beliefs. Examples of this exist in the areas of the government, the environment and education.

Problem

No Pie in the Body for "strong and powerful country".

<u>Solution:</u>   You have a choice between (1) or (2).

(1) In the **Body** you can

- put in Pie for "strong & powerful".

(2) In the **Conclusion** you can

- throw out "strong & powerful", AND
- cut back the Conclusion to cover only the items in the Introduction.

<u>...this is a country where people express many different...</u>

ADVICE BOX ON INTRODUCTION & CONCLUSION MESS-UPS

When Instructors and books tell you to "limit your Thesis", what they're trying to say is,

"Don't put anything into the Introduction, the Skeleton Summary or the Conclusion unless you have Pie for it in the Body."

Simple, huh?

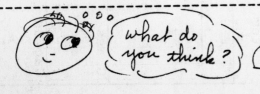

141

Organization patterns: problem & solution

There are three basic organization patterns that Instructors use in their teaching. They are the

- Unit organization
- Comparative organization
- Jumping G-B's organization.

The problem is that most students → don't recognize them, or don't know what to do with them.

Either situation will result in lowering your grade.

We'll use the material of this chart to show the three organization patterns.

GREEN PLANTS

Item → TYPES	STRUCTURE = G-B	CHARACTERISTICS = G-B	LOCATION = G-B	FUNCTION (ROLES) = G-B
Trees	- trunk - branches - bark - leaves	- trunk large rela- \tive to branches - long time to grow	- forest	- to feed deer - to give off oxygen O_2 \to atmosphere
Grass	- slender - short	- green color - perennial	- grassland	- to feed cows - to give off oxygen O_2 \to atmosphere
Cactus	- thick - short - prickles on \outside	- filled with \H_2O (water)	- desert	- to feed its animals - to give off oxygen O_2 \to atmsophere

142

In the UNIT ORGANIZATION, one item is dealt with completely before the next one is taken up. After an Introduction, all the tree information will be completed before the grass information is mentioned. And that will be finished before the cactus is brought onto the page.

In the COMPARATIVE ORGANIZATION, each G-B is dealt with completely before the next one is taken up. After an Introduction, all the structure information will be completed before the characteristics are mentioned. That will be completed before location is mentioned, and location will be completed before functions are brought onto the page.

UNIT ORGANIZATION

Introduction: "In order to find some similarities and differences between green plants, this paper will deal with three types: trees, grass and cactus."

Body:

trees	grass	cactus
- struc	- struc	- struc
- char	- char	- char
- loc	- loc	- loc
- fnc	- fnc	- fnc

Optional: statements of the similarities & differences you found. If they are not given in the Body, they must be given in the Conclusion.

Conclusion: "In conclusion, the three types of green plants--trees, cactus and grass-- are more different than alike. They have two ecological functions in common, but they are very different in where they are found, and in their characteristics and structures."

COMPARATIVE ORGANIZATION

Introduction: "In order to find some similarities and differences between green plants, this paper will deal with the structure, characteristics, location and functions of three types of green plants."

Body:

structure	char	loc	fnc
- trees	- trees	- trees	- trees
- grass	- grass	- grass	- grass
- cactus	- cactus	- cactus	- cactus

Optional: If, for reasons of length of the paper, you want to put into the Body a unit presentation of the information on any item, it can be done here.

Conclusion:

(same as Unit organization)

THE JUMPING G-B's

In this organization
the G-B's in the Body have no pattern.
They jump around all over the place.

An Instructor who has the Jumping G-B's may start
with an Introduction, or end with a Conclusion, that is
like those in the Unit or Comparative organizations.

But there is no pattern to the Body. First you're
hearing about trees, then you're getting the
characteristics of grass, etc., then you're hearing
all about cactus...

trees	char	cactus	fnc
- struc	- grass	- fnc	- trees
- loc	- cactus	- loc	- grass
- fnc	- trees	- struc	

It's very confusing.

IT IS IMPORTANT TO KNOW

✓ If your Instructor gives information in Unit organziation,

   the exam question will ask you to COMPARE the material.

✓ If you get the information in Comparative organization,

   the exam question will ask you to pull together all the
   information ON A SINGLE TOPIC (Unit organization).

✓ If you're getting the Jumping G-B's organization,

   the exam question will ask you for EITHER a Comparative
   or a Unit organization answer.

✓ If you chart your material,
   you're ready for either kind of question on the stuff.

What you want to do:

. Take down the information however it comes.
. Recognize the Instructor's organizational pattern so
            \you know the kind of question you'll be asked.
. In your Fix-ups, change the information into a pattern your
            \mind likes, & always chart when you can.

(Next page...some general exam advice.)

GENERAL ADVICE BOX FOR EXAMS

.As soon as you get your exam, glance through it to the end.

   It might have a 20-minute essay question tacked onto it at the end, and you have to allow time to answer it.

.Read the directions. Carefully. St-Pie them.

   If there is an answer sheet, read the directions for using it. And follow the directions. An out-of-place answer = zero credit. Check yourself every 5 questions.

.Read each question. Carefully.

   Use scratch paper (show it to the Instructor when you come into the exam) to make scribble notes.

   Answers that say "all", "always", "none", "never", etc., like people who say all, always, none, never, etc., are often wrong.

   Questions with "except" or "not" in them are sometimes confusing. Better re-check your answer.

.Proceed through the exam from beginning to end.

   Answer the questions you know, and put an I-will-return mark beside the questions you can't answer.

      .In multiple choice questions, read the stem of the question with EACH of the choices you are given.

         As you read, mark each choice with: (X) if it's wrong, a check mark if it's right, and a (?) if you don't know. When you come back to it, you only have to re-read the (?) choices.

   When you get to the end, start at the beginning again. Go after the unanswered, MARKED questions.

      When you answer one, scratch out the mark.

   Repeat the procedure until your time is up.

It might help... anyway, they'll get A's now. Right?

Well. It depends...

It depends on WHAT?!!?

10

IF YOU'RE THINKING ABOUT REALLY HIGH GRADES

Well, okay. I'll do the Pie first.
It's easier to explain.

There are two kinds of Pie ⤳ General Pie
&
Action or Fact Pie.

The people who mostly use
General Pie get lower grades than the ones who use Action/Fact Pie.

The Instructors don't like General Pie
as much as they like Action & Fact Pie.

They say the General Pie is "too vague",
or "too general", or "not specific enough".
They don't like it.

That's their problem.

For example,
if you say ⤳ "Mrs. Skwitch is a kind person. She does
volunteer work at the hospital and in the
community."

⤳ That's general Pie.

If you say ⤳ "Mrs. Skwitch is a kind person. She works as a
Volunteer Tutor nine hours a week in the high-
school wing of The Children's Hospital. She also
spends one afternoon each week answering the
hotline at the Community Services Center."

⤳ That's Action/Fact Pie.

Like this ⤳

```
 ┌─────────────────────────────────────────────────────────────────┐
 │  WITHOUT ACTION/FACT PIE         WITH ACTION/FACT PIE             │
 │                                                                   │
 │  Mrs. S. is a very kind person                                    │
 │    - volunteer work at hospital                                   │
 │      - ← - - - - - - - - - - - - - high-school wing of            │
 │                                        \City Hospital             │
 │      - ← - - - - - - - - - - - - - tutors 9 hours a week          │
 │    - volunteer in community                                       │
 │      - ← - - - - - - - - - - - - - answers hotline                │
 │      - ← - - - - - - - - - - - - - 1 afternoon a week             │
 └─────────────────────────────────────────────────────────────────┘
```

And like this

```
 ┌─────────────────────────────────────────────────────────────────┐
 │  WITHOUT ACTION/FACT PIE         WITH ACTION/FACT PIE             │
 │                                                                   │
 │  The seas are in trouble                                          │
 │    - rivers w/ industrial waste                                   │
 │              \flow to seas                                        │
 │      - ← - - - - - - - - - - - contain lead, arsenic, etc.        │
 │      - ← - - - - - - - - - - - approx. 1 million tons/year        │
 │    - coastal cities pump sewage                                   │
 │              \into seas                                           │
 │      - ← - - - - - - - - - - - London, Bremen, Calcutta, etc.     │
 │      - ← - - - - - - - - - - - approx. 1 million tons/year        │
 │    - fish = amount decreasing                                     │
 │      - world using more fish                                      │
 │        - world population rise                                    │
 │      - ← - - - - - - - - - - - 1930 = 2,008,000,000 people        │
 │      - ← - - - - - - - - - - - 1976 = 4,000,000,000 people        │
 │      - ← - - - - - - - - - - - 2010 = 8,000,000,000 people        │
 └─────────────────────────────────────────────────────────────────┘
```

...What you can figure is ⌐

↳if you go far enough into the
  St-Pie indent level,

⌐→ you'll get into Action/Fact Pie.

But you might not want
to study enough to get there.

So you won't get the high grade.
See?

I told you so.

If your mind doesn't absorb that kind
of Pie, there's no point in killing yourself
trying to get it.

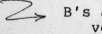 B's and C's are very,
      very okay survival grades.

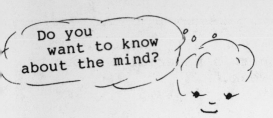

Well...besides the Pie,
        the really high grades also depend
        on the kind of mind you've got,

                what you see in the material.
                That is, the analytical ability of your mind.

        St-Pie, the G-B's and
        all the other things in this
        book
                help increase the analytical ability of your mind.

                That's why your grades improve.

Let's suppose your Instructor
handed out these notes in class.

Country X

  1712 - King dismisses Parliament
             - reason: Parliament refuses new taxation on Nobles
  1713 - King orders new taxation on Nobles
  1714 - Nobles kill tax collectors
             - silent agreement between Nobles
             - refuse to give evidence against each other
  1715 - King sends army to collect taxes
             - battles with the Nobles
                 - castles burned
                 - crops destroyed
                     - result: Peasants suffer
  1716 - Peasant uprising against Nobles
  1717 - Nobles rise up against King
         - Nobles capture King
         - Nobles establish own Parliament
             - put a limit on their taxation

Country Z

  1835 - Parliament dismisses itself
             - in order not to increase taxes on people for King
  1836 - King yields to Parliament
             - agrees to limit on taxation of the people
  1838 - Parliament changes voting rights
             - limits all powers of King and Nobles

Your Instructor now says, ⌐
                         └→"We (meaning you) will have a
                            question on this material in your
                            test next week."

        And you do ═┐
                    └→"Contrast and compare the situation in
                       Country X during the 18th century with
                       that of Country Z during the 19th century."

Okay. You're not worried.
It's no problem to recall the notes

            because you memorized them with
            Units-of-4 and scribble notes.

   So all you have to do now is write
                       it with the theme organization.

                                        Easy as Pie.

Your Thesis Sentence: Both Country X and Country Z had strong
                         disagreements between their Kings and
                         their Parliaments.
Your Skeleton Summary: Country X had one in the 18th century;
                         Country Z had one in the 19th century.

                              (Your notes are the Pie in the Body.)
Your probable grade: C

You don't like that grade? Okay. Look at your notes again.
Those disagreements resulted in very profound changes...they
were really revolutions...revolutions bring great changes...

Your Thesis Sentence: Both Country X and Country Z had important
                         revolutions between their Kings and their
                         Parliaments.
Your Skeleton Summary: Country X had one in the 18th century;
                         Country Z had one in the 19th century.

                              (Your notes are the Pie in the Body.)
Your probable grade: C+

You don't like that one either? Okay. Examine your notes
again. Those revolutions were caused by something...both
of them were about taxation...so, call them tax revolutions...

```
Your Thesis Sentence:      Both Country X and Country Z had
                           tax revolutions between their Kings
                           and their Parliaments.
Your Skeleton Summary:     Country X had one in the 18th century;
                           Country Z had one in the 19th century.

                              (Your notes are the Pie in the Body.)
Your probable grade:  B
```

You want a still higher grade? Okay, look at your notes
again. There was a difference in those tax revolutions...
one was violent, with wars and crop burnings...the other one
was managed by changing the laws. Okay, add the violence
and the law to your Thesis Sentence...

```
Your Thesis Sentence:      Both Country X and Country Z had
                           tax revolutions, but one was by violence
                           while the other took place by law.
Your Skeleton Summary:     Country X had a tax revolution by violence
                           in the 18th century; Country Z had a
                           tax revolution by law in the 19th century.

                              (Your notes are the Pie in the Body.)
Your probable grade:  B+
```

If you're going after the really high grades...

    Whether you get an A or a B
    usually depends on whether you have

            included in your Thesis Sentence
            what your Instructor thinks is "an Idea".

            An idea is an inference drawn from the facts.

            (or an implication, or an abstraction)

    Ideas are like an Instructor's personal G-B's...every
    Instructor has a different definition of what "an Idea" is.

        So, about all you can do
            is keep on making inferences and
                seeing implications, & abstracting from the material
                    until your mind doesn't see anything more.

                           151

There's one more inference that we can make
from those notes the Instructor handed out.

   Since there are tax revolutions by violence and by law,
we can infer
                    "There are different types of tax revolutions."

This inference can be your Thesis Sentence,
and we could call it "an Idea",

        because it is different than the
        inferences in the other Thesis Sentences.

   The other Thesis Sentences talk about

              what-happened and when-did-it-happen.

           But in your new Thesis Sentence,

              what-happened

                    become the Skeleton Summary.

Your Thesis Sentence: There are different types of tax
                                            revolutions.

Your Skeleton summary: Country X had a tax revolution by violence
                       in the 18th century; Country Z had a
                       tax revolution by law in the 19th century.

                        (Your notes are the Pie in the Body.

Your probable grade: A

yuck.

   The Pie used has been the same in all the answers.
   The difference in grades comes from the Thesis Sentences

Thesis Sentences		Probable Grade
X & Z = disagreements betw. King & Parl. in 18/19c.		C
" revolutions "		C+
" tax revolutions "		B
" tax rev. by violence/law "		B+
There are different types of tax revolutions.---------------		A

   So, getting high grades depends on three things

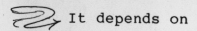 It depends on

> ↳ how much Action/Fact Pie your mind remembers,
>
> ↳ the analytical ability of your mind, and
>
> ↳ do you know how to use them both?
>
> → Will you play The Study Game?

Well, the publisher says we can't have any more space, so we have to go now.

There's an Index at the end of the book to help you find things. We hope it helps.

Goodbye. I've enjoyed the visit very much.

Goodbye. I'll always be your friend.
